FOREVER ENGLAND
North and South

FOREVER ENGLAND
North and South

Beryl Bainbridge

Duckworth/
BBC Books

Published by BBC Books
A division of BBC Enterprises Ltd
35 Marylebone High Street, London W1M 4AA
and Gerald Duckworth and Co Ltd
43 Gloucester Crescent, London NW1

First published 1987
© Beryl Bainbridge 1987

ISBN 0 563 20466 4 (cased) (BBC)

ISBN 0 7156 2097 5 (cased) (Duckworth)

British Library Cataloguing in Publication Data

Bainbridge, Beryl
    Forever England, North and South.
    1 England, Northern—Social life and
    customs 2. England—Social life and
    customs—1945—
    I. Title
    942.2'085'8   DA589.4

    ISBN 0-7156-2097-5
    ISBN 0-563-20466-4 BBC

Photoset in North Wales by
Derek Doyle & Associates, Mold, Clwyd.
Printed in Great Britain by
Robert Hartnoll (1985) Ltd., Bodmin, Cornwall

Two nations; between whom there is no intercourse and no sympathy; who are as ignorant of each other's habits, thoughts, and feelings, as if they were dwellers in different zones, or inhabitants of different planets; who are formed by a different breeding, are fed by a different food, are ordered by different manners, and are not governed by the same laws.

Disraeli, *Sybil, or The Two Nations*

Contents

Preface

This book is based on the television series, *Forever England*, which, in an attempt to examine the roots of that evergreen assumption, the notion that England is two nations, focused on the expectations and attitudes of six families, three in the North and three in the South.

The series was produced by Jimmy Dewar, directed and filmed by the cameraman John Warwick, and researched by Marie-Louise Thomas.

We rely on the evidence of written history for a knowledge of the past, and generally speaking it is a mistake to do so, for all the great events have been distorted, the important causes concealed, and most of those principal characters who figure on the page have been so misrepresented and misunderstood that the result is a complete mystification. The ordinary man, for the most part, has been left out altogether. We would do better to make our judgments on society from a study of literature, for in fiction the concept of division becomes fact – from Disraeli's *Sybil* with its subtitle 'The Two Nations' and Mrs Gaskell's *North & South*, through George Eliot, Dickens and Hardy to Lawrence's *Sons and Lovers* and the *Ragged Trousered Philanthropists* of Robert Tressel, the novel is choked with the theme of a people divided not only by borders but by circumstances of birth and opportunity.

Few of us could read in the last century, and not many of us bother to do so in this, but now we watch television, and the absurd fact is that, simply because we are presented with images rather than words, we believe that what we are watching is absolute and that the picture is complete.

It seems to me that in the end the process of making programmes, even documentary ones, is not that much different from the writing of fiction. There is landscape and dialogue, inclusion and omission. And why not? In every human character and transaction there is a mixture of humility and humbug; a little exaggeration, a little suppression; a judicious shifting of responsibility. The truth for every one of us, whether we be on the screen or in front of it, is always subjective.

h James Arstork

Introduction

I left the North of England when I was sixteen and ran away
to London, taking with me in a brown carrier bag from
Lewis's my best skirt and jumper, a box of paints, my ration
books and a framed photograph of Rasputin. I had
thirty-five shillings wrapped up in a hankie in my
mackintosh pocket.

A man I later married saw me off on the coach at midnight
down by the pier-head. He had a beard and he wore a
navy-blue duffel coat. He was balancing on the tramlines
and smiling as the moments passed; he was glad to see the
back of me. I was eating an apple and staring at him as
though I disliked him, but this was because I loved him and
thought I should never see him again in all my life.

When he said good-bye he thrust a book into my hands;
then, arms held out as though he moved a hundred feet
above the ground, he skimmed away in that hooded coat
along the tight-rope of the tram-lines. He took with him
absolutely everything – including the past in which we had
met every day.

I knew he wouldn't look back, but I turned and faced the
river as if I had already forgotten him. I blinked so hard that
the lights of New Brighton jumped like sparks. Only the
week before my father had taken me down to the landing
stage and delivered one of his lectures. He had ranted of
sailing ships forced to wait a dozen tides before floating out
on to the Mersey, of the construction of the docks, of
cholera, of how the monopolies of the great trading
companies, the Hudson Bay, the East India, the Royal

Africa, had been broken. He had real tears in his eyes – it was not just the action of the wind. He reeled off their names like a litany, and yet he was a man who believed it was heresy to vote anything other than Labour, who took pride in earning his money through commission and profit while using his franchise to put himself out of business – though sometimes he admitted to having the best of both worlds; an easy conscience and a comfortable assurance that the revolution would be a long time coming. He spoke of my paternal grandfather who had been born in 1841 and come from God knows where, of how by the time my grandfather was a man the value of goods exported from Liverpool had risen from 25 to 35 million pounds.

And yet, as my father expounded, Liverpool wasn't important industrially; there were no large factories or significant commercial enterprises other than those concerned with the shipping-trade. Less than five per cent of the population was engaged in manufactures, and though the city's growth had been connected with the rest of Lancashire, its social structure was quite different from that of the manufacturing towns. Its civic fathers, its wealthiest and most influential citizens were merchants and therefore members of the ruling classes of the nineteenth century. Unlike the Titus Salts of the time, and the Cadburys and Montague Burtons and Willses of a later era whose wealth depended on the health and passivity of a contented workforce, the seafaring men and casual labour employed on the docks had little to do with the continuing prosperity of the Liverpool merchants. The poor, who mostly lived in the Toxteth Park area between Windsor Street and the river, could afford to be ignored because they weren't of any use. When my grandfather was a lad the average age at death in Toxteth was seventeen years. Disraeli's 'Two Nations' existed in Liverpool in a more real sense than anywhere else in England. Much of the increase in population was due to those thousands fleeing from the bogs of Ireland who arrived not to settle but in hopes of moving on to the New World, only to remain trapped and impoverished in the Old. My father thought the Irish a feckless lot — the poor too, for that matter — but that was because he was a Protestant and his sister Nellie had once been propositioned outside Belmont Road Hospital by a tipsy dray-man from Galway.

I said that Malcolm Lowry had been born across the water, but my father wasn't interested. Even if he had heard of Lowry he wouldn't have had any truck with someone who came from New Brighton. He swung me round and pointed at St Nicholas's church, at the offices of the Mersey Docks and Harbour Board, at the vast edifice of the Royal Liver Building, that monument to his beloved commerce, its twin towers set with clocks like full moons and those giant birds, green wings raised, tethered under the flying clouds. 'Consider,' he bellowed, 'the advantages of cast iron.'

I said, as I had said many times before, that I was leaving home and he said, as he always did, 'Aw, chickie, what do you want to do a daft thing like that for?'

He was a travelled man himself, having gone all over the country about his business of buying and selling. He'd been in property and in cotton, safety matches and scrap metal, cork and tin-plate. Once, he'd got hold of a consignment of shoes, all size three, and I'd had to take them into school with me, in case any of my friends could be persuaded to buy them. They cost fourteen shillings a pair and were made of synthetic leather; they had a peculiar smell and I don't know which was worse, hawking them round the playground or telling my Dad that nobody liked them. For a while, during the period of the Black and Tans, he'd lived in Dublin. When he was dealing in diamonds he'd visited Amsterdam and stayed three nights in a hotel that stood in a canal. My mother too was hardly a provincial girl; her father had sent her to finishing school in Belgium. She spoke French and could play the piano — 'two blasted accomplishments', as my father often remarked when he was

13

in a black paddy, 'essential to a housewife in the North of England'. Even so, he was well over thirty when he took to the road, and my mother at twenty had been escorted to the boat-train by my grandfather's clerk. Neither of my parents wanted me to go away from home, but then, how could they stop me? You couldn't even shut the doors in our house they were so warped from the damp, let alone lock them.

To leave the North was an act of betrayal as well as folly. In the South they rode to hounds and went to Ascot; in the North we kept pigeons and raced greyhounds. When we had our tea, people in London sat down to their dinner dressed up as if they were off out to a Masonic hot-pot supper. Why, the princesses didn't have their hair permed until they were well out of ankle socks, and most of our mothers would have been ashamed for us to be seen on a Sunday in the dowdy little coats they wore every day. You could move into a street in the South and nobody would even glance in your direction until you grew old and were carried out in a coffin, and even then they wouldn't bother to remove their bowler hats as you passed. A respectable young girl could go off to the typing pool after breakfast and be sucked into the white slave trade by dinner time, never to be heard of again. We knew such home-truths from going to the pictures on a Saturday night.

All the same, these simplistic myths, matters of manners and money and location, never for one moment obscured the real differences that separated us, hid the severing wound that well-nigh cut us in half and could never be healed, for hadn't we been plundered by the South, laid waste, bled white? It was not just industrial. They had drained away our talent and our brains; who had ever heard of anyone once they had got on in the world, from William Gladstone to Thomas Handley, who had been content to stay in the North? We learnt this from our parents.

There was a further division too, this time among ourselves, nothing to do with the South: that of class. Bless the squire and his relations, keep us in our proper stations. My family knew its station all right – we weren't higher than the angels but we were up there with the vicar and the doctor and the schoolmaster. Why else was I dispatched to the chip-shop only after it had grown dark, a pudding basin in a basket on the handlebars of my bike?

We didn't much care how they lived down South, or how they fared. They had suffered during the war just as we had. But then, it seemed impossible that anyone should feel for a remote country as they would feel for their own town, their own street; that they should grieve for a disaster in which a thousand people whom they had never known had died as they would grieve for that one death in the family next door to their own.

At school we were taught history and it was about as useful to us as the study of Plato's *Republic* or the *Utopia* of More. We knew about Arthur and his cakes, Canute and his waves, and that long procession of Tudor kings, queens and princes who drifted from throne to scaffold as easily as shadows across an orchard. We took in Henry VIII and nobody told us that in the middle of all that beheading and wife-swopping the greatest barrier of all, language, the English of London which had begun with Chaucer and was itself a mixture of southern dialects, was already under construction. Five hundred years later standard English was essential if you wanted to better yourself, and some of us were sent to elocution classes to master it.

I didn't need to say that I was going to London; it was taken for granted. If you were leaving home there was nowhere else to go. And if I had told anyone that I was going down South, anyone at all – my music teacher, the farmer across Bumpy Fields, the porter at the station – they'd have known I meant London. The North stretched from Birmingham to Newcastle and then became Scotland. The South was one place, one city. Devon and Cornwall were seaside resorts; Surrey and Somerset and Suffolk and all the rest of those distant counties were simply places to which people went on holiday. They didn't count. The real and only 'down South' was London.

I remember it was cold the night I left, and blustery, the wind blowing in from the Irish Sea. I could hear the river slapping up against the harbour wall like a dog lapping water. It was a good thing, the weather being so melancholy and the hour so late. Who wants one's heart to break on a morning filled with sunlight?

When the coach started and we drove towards Castle Street I looked for that figure in the duffel coat, but there was only an old man pushing a ha..d .art into the shadow of Queen Victoria sitting dumpy and offended on her throne above the lamplight, her knees chipped by bomb blast and the coiled hair on her stone neck silvery with the droppings of gulls. I opened the book I had been given and read its title. It was the life of Benvenuto Cellini; on the fly-leaf, scrawled in pencil, were the words 'Until tomorrow'.

I cried all the way to Warrington until a man in a camel-hair coat got on to the coach and sat down next to me. He switched off the overhead light and covered both our laps with a plaid rug. He didn't speak to me. He interfered with me all the way to Knutsford and I was too polite to protest – it was quite kind, sharing the rug.

We passed through dormant villages where invisible branches raked the windows, and plunged into towns where people never slept and the factories and the foundries blazed all night, smoke stacks belching against the moon. At Stratford-on-Avon we stopped for half an hour. I bought a cheese sandwich and ate some of it standing on a bridge above the river and threw the rest of it at a dingy swan that came gliding out of the darkness below; even the bread tasted different down South. I thought I knew what I was leaving behind and I never doubted that I could go back and that it would all be exactly as I had left it.

A mistake, of course, just as it's a mistake to think that the past can ever be scuttled and forgotten. For a while, perhaps, we may succeed in submerging those memories and influences of lost and bygone days, until, jolted by a fragment of melody, a view glimpsed from a speeding train, some words scribbled in the margin of a book, they will rise unbidden to the surface, bringing up the past with such insistence that we well may choke on it.

1

The Macleans of Liverpool

It took longer than expected to get to the first pub because the taxi driver had forgotten that concrete blocks had been set along the top of the road to cause a diversion. We had to keep going round and round what was left of the houses to find an escape route.

It didn't matter about the delay. We weren't meeting the rest of the family until eight o'clock and it was not yet seven.

I asked Rosie if she thought they would all turn up and she said we would have to take pot luck.

George said, 'Get away, they'll all be there, girl.' I told him that my father had been the youngest of nine.

'Deborah,' I said, 'Nellie, Margaret, Jack, Sally who died of a broken heart, Jim, Frederick and Harold.'

I made up the last three. There had been nine of them, but my father had never been able to remember the names of his elder brothers. It was true about Sally; she had gone into a decline after her sweetheart came back gassed from France and died on the steps of Alder Hay Hospital. George and Rosie showed polite interest – compared with their own family such numbers were hardly spectacular.

The driver said it was a blasted assault course driving through this part of Liverpool. He was separated from his passengers by a metal grille so that nobody could hit him over the head with a bottle. Anywhere else one might have supposed that the blocks had been put down to make the area more pleasant, less hazardous for pedestrians; in this case it was more probable that they were positioned to hinder car thieves and burglars from making a getaway. I could be wrong. I do know that five years ago, for that very reason, they made a similar adjustment to the road outside the new housing estate in Upper Stanhope Street, shortly before they planted saplings on the waste ground behind

Faulkner Square – though that was to deter residents from throwing bricks at policemen on mild summer nights.

It's painful returning to a place that is always being demolished and refurbished. The past, which is a state of mind rather than an accumulation of time, is liable to suffer disturbance when its boundaries are destroyed. Everything becomes topsy-turvy; in dreams I can walk down those once familiar streets but when I'm awake I can't find them.

My father-in-law, who was considered wealthy as well as middle-class, used to live in a house off Faulkner Street. His neighbours were surgeons and sculptors and cotton merchants. He wore a monocle in his glass eye, having lost the real one in the First World War leaning out of his aeroplane to drop bombs on the bosch at St Amand. At Christmas he threw fancy-dress parties during which ornaments got broken. His background or his education had given him different aspirations from those of my parents, both of whom insisted that if you paid them good money they wouldn't be caught dead living in one of those draughty mausoleums in the slums of Liverpool. They belonged to another class whose particular castle stood in the suburbs in the shape of a new bungalow, a bank manager over the garden fence on one side, a shipping clerk on the other, and a tea-party round a brass tray on an Indian table in the lounge one Sunday afternoon in a lifetime. Their preference for the new had something to do with an abhorrence of second-hand property, of whatever sort. Old houses were similar to old clothes in that one could never be sure who had last been seen in them. My mother wouldn't even countenance second-hand furniture, employing instead a cabinet-maker to reproduce copies of things she admired. She was proud of the Jacobean chest, the George IV mahogany table, the six Queen Anne chairs, all made in Southport in 1931. It could be that she was suffering from a childhood stuffed with hand-me-down goods. My father boasted of having attended St Emmanuel's church school,

Anfield, and of leaving it for the world of commerce, never to look back, when he was no more than nine years old. My mother kept under her hat where she was born and in what circumstances she had lived before the success of my grandfather's paint firm had catapulted her to pianoforte lessons in that continental establishment across the sea. But then, my father had risen in the world and in pin-pointing his beginnings was simply charting the distance he'd travelled. My own attachment to old buildings, my rejection of new ones, I blame on Dickens. There is nothing like reading *Bleak House* at an impressionable age in a bungalow for fixing the mind ever afterwards on garrets and cellars and aspidistras in the parlour.

At any rate, when I looked out of the window of the cab I couldn't tell where I was and it unsettled me. Pulling down the big houses and putting up little ones has somehow altered the scale of the city – the roads seem too wide, the sky too high. I complained as much to George, who said, 'Yes, you're right', in a sympathetic tone of voice, but he was humouring me. I suppose if you're on the spot and it goes on in front of your eyes, change is neither shocking nor apparent, rather like friends who see one another every day and never notice that they're growing older.

That first pub we went into was as big as a brewery and gloomy as the Black Hole of Calcutta. The light bulbs hung so close to the nicotine sheen of the brown vaulted ceiling that below we sat in rippling shadow, faces reflected in water. There was a picture of the Queen Mother, smiling, mounted on a piece of card beside the dartboard; she had puncture marks in her hat. Somewhere in the darkness they were playing billiards. I couldn't see anyone but every now and then I heard the dull little clop of a ball as it dropped into the pocket.

George wanted to leave after one drink. He said there was going to be trouble at the next table where a woman in a silver-flecked jumper was trying to stop an angry man in a donkey jacket from hitting her daughter. She kept crooking her arm about the man's neck, the pear-drop of her bony elbow luminous against the anaglypta of the wall, and he kept attempting to shake her loose, clawing at the skin of her arm with his nails as though picking off cobwebs; she was throttling him. The argument had something to do with a rent book that had gone missing. There were witnesses who could swear it had been under the milk jug after the telly had finished the night before. The woman said several times, 'You've got to see our Teresa's point of view, Jacko', and once the girl told her that she was wasting her breath. 'He's pig-ignorant, Mam,' she said. She was eating peanuts, looking at the man slyly, licking the salt from her fingers. She was angry too, but only because it made it easier to hold herself in check. If she had weakened for a moment, to the extent of uttering one soft word of appeasement, of understanding, she might have burst into tears. Already, in the expression of her eyes, the beginnings of her small triumphant smile, there was more than a touch of the martyr.

We walked to the next pub against wind and rain and heard the music even before we turned the corner by the black railings of the gutted church. Ahead of us a daisy-chain of young girls in sleeveless summer dresses, arms linked, white high-heeled shoes prinking over the puddles, broke shrieking across the road. But for the noise they made they might have been ghosts, those pale girls shimmering above the asphalt gloss of the wet, lamplit street. In an instant they had pushed back the door and engulfed in bluish vapour vanished into the Angel Vaults. 'Granddaughters,' said Rosie complacently.

Inside the musicians were playing like men possessed, amplifiers turned up full blast, the plucked notes of the electric guitar cracking the air like a whiplash. Deafened, we sat under the pink glow of paper lanterns, mouthing greetings, lip-reading names. We were all grimacing, nodding, ferociously listening. 'I like a family pub where they don't encourage conversation,' shouted George.

He introduced me to his sister Monica who with her husband had come up from Wales for the weekend. She was a handsome woman in a fur coat, big and strong-boned, graciously smiling and showing a forthright affection for her brother.

'We were up the road,' George told her, 'but we had to blow.' He nudged me confidentially. 'That other place,' he said, 'It was leading to aggro – understand what I mean?'

'It's rough up the road,' said Rosie.

Peter, her fourth son, the one coming between Christi and Terence, came and sat down beside her. He worked at Higson's brewery and he and his wife Joanie lived in the same road as his parents. Sometimes Joanie had asthma attacks and then he ran for his Mam.

'I love her bones,' he said, and he meant Rosie as well as Joanie. He'd never left Liverpool and never would. Last year he became friendly with a French photographer whose car had broken down in Northumberland Street. They got talking, and later they went out for a bevvy together, and what with one thing and another the Frenchman and his wife ended up staying in Peter's house. The photographer was loony about Liverpool, possessed you might say. He was nothing like those Japanese wallahs who arrived every summer lisping to be taken for a walk round Strawberry Fields and Abbey Road and Penny Lane; this bloke was caught up in its history, spellbound by its streets, snapping the docks and the cobblestones and the crumbling warehouses as if it was the remains of an ancient civilisation he was capturing on film. When he got back to Paris he wrote to Peter and asked him over on a visit. He never went. How could he? For one, he didn't want his likeness stuck into a passport, and for another he couldn't leave his Mam.

I would have liked to have asked Rosie if there had been times when she had gone hungry, she and all those children

living in inadequate rooms in unheated tenements, but I
didn't suppose she could reply with her hand on her heart. I
remember once telling a school friend in front of my mother
that my Auntie Nellie and my Auntie Margo were poor. My
mother snapped my head off; she said it wasn't nice to use
that word. And another time she stopped speaking to my
grandmother for weeks on end because she overheard her
confiding to me that she had worked in a lollypop factory
when she was a young girl. It wasn't nice to talk about
things like that either. My mother timed her death down to
the last penny. She left when she had spent the small
inheritance bequeathed to her by my grandfather. In the
wardrobe was her old age pension book and five pounds in
loose change. To be poor then was something that shamed
the individual. Now, shame is transferred to the State.

George was in the middle of a story about a bird, a
feathered one. I thought at first he was talking about
pigeons, but then he spanned the smoke-filled air with his
hands as though measuring an eagle. I couldn't catch the
half of it, until the band suddenly stopped for a breather and
I heard him say, '... and there was the parrot in the oven.'
Everyone nodded emphatically, swearing it wasn't a lie, and
George dug Rosie in the ribs, demanding to know if it wasn't
God's truth.

Rosie wasn't listening; she sat there, taking a back seat,
twisting the silver strap of her wrist-watch, gazing placidly
out at a room full of family. She had seven sons, four
daughters and twenty-seven grandchildren, seven of whom
had children of their own. She didn't look her age and yet
nothing remained of her youthful self, except in that way
she had of perching far back on the padded upholstery of the
bench so that her plump legs, crossed at the ankles, didn't
quite touch the floor; that, and her expression of stoic
acceptance. There was a lantern above her head but the light
fell only partly on her; she was leaning against George and
in his shadow, where perhaps she had always been.

Then the band started up again and it was time for
George's party piece. He swaggered onto the floor and stood
there, moistening his lips above the black snout of the
microphone, shoulders hunched in his smart tweed jacket,
those black eyebrows raised in mock bewilderment as he
waited for the opening bars of the refrain.

Monica told me that George had always been a fine singer.
He'd taken part in a talent contest at the Rialto ballroom
with the Billy Cotton Dance-band – he'd leapt up onto the
stage as if he didn't have a nerve in his body. She was tickled
pink, eyes beaming behind her tinted spectacles, her charm
bracelet slithering on her wrist as she fluttered her fingers to
the beat of the band.

'He could have been a star,' she said.

'I'm dancing with tears in my eyes,' sang George.

He was hesitant at first, then he got into his stride and
mimicking Jolson, wriggled down almost to his knees, arms
held out to Mammy in supplication.

'I'm dancing,' he crooned, 'yes I'm dancing, can't you see
me, can't you see I'm dancing with tears in my eyes?'

Rosie had moved to a table nearer to the centre of the
floor. She sat sideways on her chair, watching him, fiddling
with a little scrap of handkerchief as if preparing for the
rapture of her own tears. We were all watching him now; the
married men and their wives leaning companionably
shoulder to shoulder, marvelling at the cheek of him, the
courting couples holding hands, the young girls and the
clowning boys.

At the very end he held out his hand to Rosie. At first she
resisted, not wanting to make a show of herself, and then she
let him pull her to her feet and went readily enough into his
arms, clinging to him as they swayed awkwardly across the
floor.

Nothing in the world could be better than those moments,
than those half circles they performed within the wider circle
of the family.

*

As a working man, Christopher Maclean counts himself among the fortunate. With the exception of two years on the dole when he was first married, he has been employed on the docks as a boat handler for the best part of twenty years. A man has a necessity for work; it's his right. He doesn't have any respect for himself if he can't organise his life, support his own family. His eldest boy, young Chris, who is married and lives with his wife and children up the road in a decaying pre-war tenement in Dingle Mount, is employed at the moment, though there's no guarantee how long it will last. Before that he was out of work for two years, and before that he was on one of those dead-end government schemes. He got himself qualifications as a welder and just as he was about to be made up from apprenticeship to full wages, they gave him the push. It broke his heart. Tony has never had a job. Christopher understands why he can't get out of his bed until the afternoon and yet it irritates him, hearing young Tony wandering round the house in the small hours, turning night into day. Young Chris keeps a lot of misery inside him. He's never asked either of them for a penny but he gets depressed because he's an able man, a willing man who wants to work. His father got angry with him a while back – he started talking about himself as though he was a down and out, of no account or worth. It was sickening and saddening listening to him, and it was all wrong, a thoughtful responsible young man like that reduced to having such a low opinion of himself.

*

My father went out to business. Sometimes, if he was delayed by some task imposed on him by my mother, he would remark petulantly that he should be off to his work. It was a slip of the tongue; he was self employed and had business to attend to. Work implied some menial job in which he was a mere cog in the machine. A man had a right to be in business, to make his own decisions.

Miss Burns, our neighbour, who was middle-aged and lived with her swindler of a brother, went out to business as well. In her case she was a typist at the municipal offices in Bootle. Neither she nor her brother, whether they were in business or not, had any right to the house next door. Its rightful owner, Mr Rimmer, the bank manager, had been press-ganged into something hush-hush down South at the start of the war, and he had let the house to the Burnses. When the war was concluded he tried to move them out but there was some damn-fool legislation which had turned them into protected tenants and the beggars wouldn't shift. My father detested them. They wouldn't pay their whack to have the fence repaired when it blew down in the gales. They said it was Rimmer's responsibility and of course, in the circumstances, he wasn't about to cough up a brass farthing. Who could blame him? The fence was of no use to him, down or up, not when he couldn't set foot inside his own front door, let alone the garden. My father turned the hose on Mr Burns, accidentally on purpose, shortly after VE-Day and they never spoke to each other again.

Mrs Riley, across the road, had two jobs, pig keeping and piano teaching. When my brother came back from his lesson my mother made him go and hang up his blazer on the privet hedge – to get rid of the smell. Mrs Riley boiled the pig swill on the kitchen range; she went in and out to stir the peelings, sleeves rolled up to her elbows while he played his Rachmaninov prelude. As both her jobs were conducted on the premises it couldn't be said that she went out to business.

My Auntie Margo was a dressmaker and received her customers in the front parlour of the rented house in Bingley Road. For a short while during the war she worked in the munitions factory at Speke, but that was kept quiet. Years before, Auntie Nellie had been employed in some capacity at the Belmont Road hospital, in the wing for naughty girls who had to have their heads shaved and their clothes taken away from them. Auntie Margo let out that Nellie had been a cleaner there but my mother insisted that she was romancing as usual.

Naturally, my mother didn't go out to either work or business. She had enough to do painting the furniture and rearranging the ornaments. We had little figurines trembling on every window-sill and shelf, and a row of plaster dogs, painted over so often that it was no longer possible to tell which breed they resembled, stalking the narrow ledge above the picture rail in the hall. A too hastily slammed door could bring the lot down. My brother complained it was like walking through a mine-field. Everything was in its place, though never for long. We had only to grow used to the dancing girl, painted dazzling white on the dining-room mantelpiece, and she was gone, holding her skirts now dark green and luminous above the mahogany bookcase in the lounge. My father said my mother was a menace with a paintbrush; she had no self-control. If we didn't watch out she'd undercoat the lot of us to tone in with the colour of the wallpaper.

The furniture in our house was shifted round so often that we stopped talking about the lounge and the dining-room. They were only courtesy titles anyway. It hardly mattered what they were called, seeing that we never did any lounging or dining in either of them. We spent our lives cooped up in the side-room – wisely never referred to as the living-room – crawling under the table to fetch a glass of water from the scullery, fighting for space to do our homework, jostling each other as we took it in turns to get warm at the fire. If anybody called, perish the thought, my brother had to stand out in the hall. It was no use ushering visitors into the front-room; without a fire laid hours in advance, they ran the risk of frostbite. When my brother was allowed in there to do his piano practice he had to keep breaking off to rub his chilblains against the edge of the keys. If somebody did ring the front door bell we turned off the light and went quiet. We weren't fit to be seen. My mother and father kept their good clothes for the outside world. Indoors my mother wore her slip and an old suit jacket torn under the arms. My father sat engulfed in an air-raid warden's uniform which would have fitted a man twice his size.

We took holidays, which was unusual in our street, though never abroad. Nobody did, or not anybody we had ever met. The days had gone when people like my grandfather, that upright, self-improving man, who stuck pins through dried butterflies in the cramped box-room of his suburban villa in West Derby, could travel first class on a passenger steamer to Barcelona. My mother, once her continental days had passed, could no more afford to gallivant in his wake than could her own mother, who, in failing to rise from her lollypop beginnings, had been left behind in more ways than one.

My father's attitude to marriage was pessimistic. He himself had not considered it until he was almost forty. Before he met my mother on the top deck of a tram in Lord Street he had been engaged for seven years to a woman called Ann Moss — my mother nicknamed her Animosity. He lived with his widowed mother, Ellen, and his two sisters, Nellie and Margo. Nellie was a martyr who had sacrificed herself, willingly, in order to look after Mother, who was halfway between a saint and an angel. According to my mother, Ellen was one of those saints who came over queer and had to lie down whenever she was asked to do anything. My father had hopes that my mother would have her to live with them after they were married, to give Nellie her chance, but he was whistling on the wind. Margo had been briefly wed in 1915 to a soldier-boy who was buried in the mud of the trenches. She got a war widow's pension out of it. Later, during the next war, she made a spectacle of herself over a school teacher who was billeted on them and she would have married him if it hadn't been for my father and Nellie, who both accused her of giddiness, of being soft in the head at even contemplating giving up her pension.

The notion that a man should get married when young was foreign to my father. My brother would never have dared to suggest it, not until he was through university and had something in the bank, and even then there was no call to rush things. When I told him I was thinking of getting married he went to see my young man – he was nearly thirty – and tried to talk him out of it. He said I was hopeless in the home and would only be a millstone round his neck.

My father had no hobbies. He read his daily paper, subscribed to the *Statesman and Nation* and the *Windjammer* and listened to the wireless in the dark. And for a time he dug for victory. He fancied himself as a gardener, though he appeared to find more aggravation than pleasure in the occupation. He was out in all weathers in that voluminous battledress, a black beret jammed over his ears, his trousers held up with a length of elastic, cursing and groaning as he fought the elements. In winter he complained that his particular patch of England was nothing but a blasted quagmire, and he ground his teeth in fury when the warmer days came, turning the earth to a thin sand which blew from his lettuce beds and lay in drifts beneath the poplar trees at the fence.

My mother tended roses, sweet williams, dahlias. Come November the airing-cupboard rustled with wizened tubers smelling of old newspapers. She grew tomatoes in the little greenhouse beyond the washing-line where once the air-raid shelter had stood. My father dug the shelter but after only two days the foundations flooded and he filled them in again, flinging the sheets of corrugated tin and the wooden planks into the nettles of the back field. He said we would have to take our chances in the coal-hole under the stairs – a direct hit would be quicker than drowning.

When he was feeling sorry for himself he sulked in the greenhouse and we took his meals down to him on a tray. My mother said it was more convenient having him outside. Sometimes he refused to open the door and we left his tray on the grass and the dog walked all over it, whining, leaving paw marks on the mashed potatoes. When my father emerged my mother ran down the path and shoved the greenhouse door backwards and forwards on its hinges as though the air inside had been contaminated.

My father had animals to contend with as well as the weather. There were rabbits in the back field and Mrs Riley had rats because of her pigs. Our dog had a heart condition, and if it spotted a rabbit and gave chase, my father had to sit up nights with it, feeding it brandy from a spoon. Times without number the wind tore in from the sea across the flat fields, uprooting the pole of the washing line and scattering the clothes on the ground. Then, one or other of us would rush to pick up the soiled jumpers and shirts, trampling the seedlings into oblivion. Stamping his feet like an Indian on the warpath, whirling the rake above his head like a tomahawk, my father consigned us all to hell. He was not by any means one of those sons of the soil who thought he was nearer to God in a garden than anywhere else on earth. Our garden was part investment, part show; it had to be kept decent both for its property value and for the sake of the neighbours.

*

Christopher Maclean has an allotment. The house he and his wife Ann are buying on a mortgage doesn't have a garden, just a scrap of concrete yard at the back. In a tub under the front windows there's a creeper which was nipped in the bud by the frosts of last winter.

The allotment is on a ridge of land not far from the house. If it was possible to look from a height on this southern aspect of the Mersey and by some miracle to peel back time so that years passed in the space of seconds, demolishing in minutes that grand expansion of the nineteenth century, leaving nothing when the dust had lifted but a waste of common ground rising from a deserted foreshore towards a plateau of cultivated plots, one might see in that rural landscape some resemblance to the present. On a mild evening Christopher can sit on his painted bench outside his greenhouse and look clear across a river empty of ships to Bidson and the Cheshire hills beyond. Below, and further along the shoreline where once the monumental warehouses stood black against the sky, the flags of the Garden Festival site wallow in the breeze.

He comes here most evenings except Saturdays. Saturdays he goes coarse fishing on the Bridgewater canal. He enjoys both gardening and fishing, but he stresses the distinction between work and hobbies. Without a job, fooling about with a rod and line, digging the earth, however pleasurable, would only remind him that he had time on his hands.

He grows vegetables: kale and beetroot, onions, cabbages, swedes. Last year when he went on holiday to the continent he brought back a strain of Spanish tomato. This year he tried sweet-corn, without much luck. The weather's been too wet. He has a few flowers: sweet peas climbing up the wire netting by the compost-heap, roses, marigolds – nothing too ambitious. He's going to get rid of the sweet peas – they may look good but they encourage mice. The allotment isn't his, not yet. At present it's leased to an old fellow, a Canadian from Newfoundland who's a bit on the frail side now and hasn't been down to keep an eye on things for three years. Christopher sees to it that he doesn't go short of produce.

Sometimes in the summer when she has finished her shift as an orderly at the Royal Liverpool Hospital, Ann comes here to sit with him. It's a break for her. They're both 'made up' with the house and they've devoted time and money to stripping the woodwork of the doors and staircase and generally making improvements, but it's still on the cramped side. They began married life in an attic – the kitchen was in the cellar and they brought up most of their children on the third floor of a tenement in Brunswick Gardens so they're not complaining, just surprised that they're still short on space.

Ann and he grew up in the same street and went to the same school. She too came from a large Catholic family. They both left school at fifteen and married at nineteen. They have five children and four grandchildren, one of whom, Ann-Marie's baby, lives with them. In early middle-age they both can't help thinking of the day when at last they'll have the house to themselves. The baby will be walking soon and then there'll be all that business of putting the ornaments out of his reach and setting a chair at the foot of the stairs to keep him out of mischief. It's lovely having a baby in the house and they think the world of him, but after Colette they had thought they were done with that sort of responsibility. His Mam has the same problem. Often you can't get through the front door of Rosie's house for the daughters and the grandchildren lying about like gold dust. Little Bernard, Peter and Joanie's boy, the one who sucks his milk through a teat on a vinegar cruet, stays nights with his Gran at the little palace. It's that old dilemma: if you come from a big family you think heaven is a bit of time to yourself, a bit of space, and yet when it comes to it and they all shove off and the house is tidy for once, and shining, all you feel is lost and time is a burden. Not that he and Ann have arrived at that watershed, nor Rosie for that matter.

He worries about the future for his sons, Tony and young Chris in particular. Gary and Colette are still at school. For the last two years a wonderful thing has been happening in Liverpool 8. All sorts of people have come forward to help the children; teaching them dancing and music and coaching them at sports, making them take it seriously, talking to them about diet and fitness and dedication. And it's all voluntary work; they don't receive a penny in recompense. All the same, it doesn't help Tony and young Chris. What Liverpool needs is some money or a different government. That Woman frowns on the working class; she'd like to see them stamped into the ground. If her footwear matched her intentions she'd never be seen without her gum-boots. Some people blame it on the Common Market, the decline of trade. Others, the management class, naturally, on the so-called belligerence of the dockers. Wherever the fault lies That Woman certainly isn't helping. She'd like to see them all starved into submission. Look what happened to his Dad when he went into business for himself and ran his own haulage firm, employing other blokes and showing initiative. He was squeezed out by things like Value Added Tax and high interest rates and all the rest of it. What was the point of George slogging his guts out just to give it back to the government? It could swing back, if there was investment. Something has to be done. Out of his six brothers only Terence and Peter were working. Tommy, George, Michael and Bernard were all on the dole. For the best part of the day he himself had been working in the hold of a Greek ship berthed at the Alexandra Dock, unloading cattle-food from Pakistan. He couldn't pretend it hadn't been a messy job, standing amid that blizzard of rice grain, togged up in a white balaclava and goggles like Captain Scott on his way to the pole. Even with a mask over his nose it was impossible not to inhale some of the stuff. Tomorrow, if there was nothing doing at the Alexandra Dock he could be sent further along the front to the containers at Seaforth.

He said life was all right for him. He had his family, his allotment and a drink on a Saturday night after the fishing. What more could a man ask for, as long as he was in work. It was the young he pitied. His generation had been brought up hard. The young had had an easier time of it and now it was getting worse they couldn't handle it. They had nothing to look back on; they didn't remember how it was.

*

Every Friday my father came home from his business and filling up the tank of his Wolseley car with the black-market petrol he kept in an oil drum in the coal-hole under the stairs, drove back into town to buy the weekend joint from his nephew Jack, who kept a butcher's shop off the Priory Road. Afterwards he went to St John's Market for a bit of fish for the tea. He said my mother was a poor housekeeper with no idea of budgeting; she said that that was rich, him going all that way for a lump of pork and a piece of cod she could have fetched in ten minutes from the village. She didn't like him seeing his relations. She thought he came back different, tainted by a past she wanted to forget.

Sometimes I was allowed to go with him. At the beginning of the war he and I had been caught in an air-raid. I don't remember it but my mother described it so often that I thought I did. We had been coming back along the dock road when the sirens went. My father cursed, putting his foot down hard on the accelerator, trying to put distance between himself and the town. Behind us the searchlights sliced the bloated bellies of the barrage balloons. The car skidded on a slick of oil and a pound of apples lodged on the shelf under the polished dashboard burst their bag and cannoned about the seats. According to my mother, my father felt as though he had been caught in crossfire. He thought his number was up and had held up his hands in surrender. Even so, I set up such a caterwauling whenever I saw him go into the coal-hole that mostly she let me go.

Once through the woods at Ince Blundell and over the bridge by the biscuit factory we were well on the way to Bootle and the dock road which stretched from Seaforth Sands in the north to the oil storage cliffs of the old Herculaneum Dock in the south. My father had been in shipping before the First World War, exporting some

37

mysterious commodity to the continent. Though it was difficult to believe, given his wilting flower attitude in later life to draughts, his sensitivity of mind and stomach, he had sailed as a boy before the mast on a brig to Boston and back. Then, there was trade with the Indies and the Brazils, the Africas and the Americas. The warehouses were stuffed with tobacco and tea, sugar, cotton and salt; the air thick with the sweet-sour smell of bonded rum and grain. On the overhead railway the wooden carriages rocked above the water, past the Alexandra Dock and the Huskisson, the Canada, Princes and Georges, the Albert, Salthouse, Brunswick, Toxteth and Harrington. You could identify the shipping lines by the colours they flew from the masted boats stuck in the black jelly of river – the Ellerman, the Allen, Cunard, Blue Funnel, White Star. If a man had a mind to he could embark for Calcutta or San Antonio, Leghorn and Genoa, Jamaica or New York. The road was desperate with traffic; coal trucks and timber wagons and brewers' carts with iron wheels dragged thundering over the cobblestones by dray-horses the size of elephants. Three times a week the cattle were transported on hydraulic lifts from ship to quay and herded up the hill to the abattoir. Yet beneath that bright and busy world lay a dark underside of poverty and drunkenness, cruelty and death. Some men fared little better than the cattle, their lives but a brutal run from the cradle to the grave.

By now my father would have his handkerchief out, ready for an emotional blowing of his nose. He was leading up to the saintly Ellen who had reared him. Others, he would tell me, poor though their homes might be, were nurtured by good and decent mothers who wore their fingers to the bone cleaning and washing and darning, disciplining by example rather than by the rod. I was always slightly uneasy at this point. I was never sure that he wasn't getting at my mother under cover of praising his own, though mine had never gone for me with so much as a feather duster. Little homes, he would continue, modest yet clean, in which the warmth of love burned brighter than any fire.

On the opposite side of the road, a public house, a mission hall and a provision shop on every corner, the mean courts climbed towards the rose-pink cathedral whose Protestant bells rang out on a Sunday morning, deafening the Catholic inhabitants of the grim little houses which stood in its shadow, until, reaching the brow of the hill the roads broadened out into the once prosperous thoroughfares of Rodney Street and Canning Street, Huskisson and Upper Parliament, to Princes Boulevard and Sefton Park where once the cotton kings had strolled.

We stopped at Bingley Road to call in on my Aunties. I liked going there. Auntie Nellie stored women's magazines under the cushions of the sofa in case Auntie Margo had to keep one of her customers waiting. Sometimes I stayed the night with them. When they got ready for bed they put their flannel nightgowns on over their clothes. They grunted and twisted on the hearth rug, struggling to undo the numerous hooks of their undergarments; at last, panting and triumphant they tore free the great pink stays and dropped them to the floor, where they stood stiffly upright, shaped like cricket pads, the little dangling suspenders sparkling in the firelight. I slept between my aunts; in winter the green silk counterpane lay cold as glass on my mouth.

Auntie Nellie made my father lie down on the sofa as soon as he set foot through the door. She said he ought to conserve his strength. They were much poorer than us, but when we had our tea the cups and saucers matched and they had a sugar bowl as well as a milk jug. At home my mother dumped the sugar bag and the milk bottle alongside the wireless on the window-sill. My aunts paid fourteen shillings a week for the house which was in a road half way between the Lune Laundry and the Cabbage Hall. It came nearer to my ideal of a Dickensian dwelling than any other place I knew. Outside the back door a little slope of yard led to an alleyway and an outhouse where they kept the mangle and the dolly-tub. I knew without being told that I mustn't mention back home that we'd popped in to Bingley Road. My mother suspected my father of giving money to his sisters, and it infuriated her, the thought of him throwing his money away on them when she had to beg for every shilling of housekeeping. She said it wasn't right the way Margo let me read those ridiculous old love-letters sent her by that long-dead soldier boy, and what possible interest could I have in that photograph album stuck full of faded strangers.

St John's Market was in Elliot Street. We parked the car round the corner in Williamson Square. That was after we had bought the meat. I didn't care for my cousin Jack or my Uncle John. When my Uncle John saw me he made me tap-dance on the sawdust spot because he knew I went to dancing classes. He said I had bonny legs. On a bad day I had to sing 'Kiss me Goodnight, Sergeant-major', my cousin Jack in his bloody apron thumping the chopping board with his cleaver to give me a beat. There was the head and shoulders of a pig on the shelf beneath the clock. It looked more like a simpering girl than a porker, with its stiff yellow eyelashes, its coquettish shoulders rounded above its cut-off trotters.

In Williamson Square the black-shawled flower-sellers sat on upturned crates beside the wrought-iron public conveniences. The caught-short men ran with fumbling fingers and stood in the open air to relieve themselves, the bottoms of their trousers showing and their boots splayed out to avoid the drizzle. Sometimes a hand with a fistful of daffodils or an upturned umbrella would rise above the crenellated rims of the circular urinals.

It was embarrassing watching my father shop. His contemptuous expression made it appear that the transaction was beneath him, and yet, the way he haggled over its price, you might have thought he was buying a whale rather than that wretched piece of cod. When he was handed his change he turned the coppers over in his palm, examining them, doing everything but bite them before replacing them in his pocket. He bought me a cake at the stall but he wouldn't let me eat it out of the paper bag. I whined that I could use a plate provided by the stall and he protested that I might catch a disease. One would have thought he was made of something rarer, finer than flesh and blood the way he drew back like an offended maiden when a poor and smelly boy pressed too close to him; the disgust on his face when he saw what he called a 'wicked woman' accosting a man. He squatted there on his haunches, ramming a wodge of newspaper between the lump of pork and the slice of fish in the carrier bag at his feet, tut-tutting under the singing gas-mantles of that beautiful long-gone market.

At the time I suspected him of being a snob, in spite of his socialist principles. The rules he lived by, the comical distinctions between what was nice and not nice, the thrift he practised, switching off the lights as if liquid gold leaked from the bulbs, rationing the bath water. The pretensions: the hats and coats and shiny shoes we faced the world in when there was but one moulting toothbrush in the cracked mug in the bathroom and not a single pair of pyjamas in the airing cupboard; the pampered furniture arranged on the good carpet in the arctic wastes of that unused front-room, the scuffed utility table sliding on that rag of a string mat in the side-room; the blackened knives and the bent forks in the scullery drawer and the silver cutlery in the green leather case atop the tall-boy.

Only later did I come to understand that my father was keeping up appearances. His money went on school fees and school books, hockey-sticks and tennis-rackets, the *National Geographic Magazine;* on Latin coaching and extra French, elocution tuition, dancing classes and music lessons. If we were forbidden to play with the evacuee children billeted over the railway line it was because he was paying with the sweat of his brow to put distance between us and them. Desperate lest we should slip and join the common herd from which he came, he would push us all the way up that slippery, expensive ascent whether we appreciated it or not.

If he had lived long enough to experience the prosperity of the last two decades his fear would have abated, lulled by the emergence of cheap and stylish clothing, the accessibility of hot water and soap. Today, if he walked the streets of his native city he would sense again the dangerous presence of the dispossessed.

My mother too lived in mortal terror of the powerful past. When my Auntie Margo died, leaving me the contents of the house in Bingley Road, my mother telephoned to ask what I wanted to keep. I said I didn't mind about the furniture, that I was only interested in the letters and the photographs. Before I got there she wangled the key out of the next-door neighbours and took the bottom drawer of the wardrobe into the backyard. Tipping the letters and the snapshots into a metal bin she made a bonfire of the lot.

When my parents died the roof of our house was waterproof, the window-frames sound. It was their legacy to their children.

*

Young Chris Maclean and his wife Gwyneth are moving to a new house in the near and hopeful future. Some five years ago the tenants of Dingle Mount formed themselves into a co-operative and with the help of an architect began to design their own housing estate. When Chris was on the dole the planning of it helped to keep him sane. At first his house didn't have a chimney and when he looked at the drawings he thought something was missing, not quite right. He asked the architect if he could have a chimney instead of a porch. He knew he couldn't have both because of the costing. Some of the other tenants, having seen his chimney, decided to have one too, even though there'll be gas-fires in the grates.

He says that at the risk of sounding like a robot all he wants is his own house and a little garden. It won't actually be his; he'll be renting it, but he'll have his own front door and his own plot of grass. As soon as the gardens get started his father will be down to advise on fertilisers and planting. At the moment the foundations are laid and the first storeys are going up. They hold meetings every week to discuss the sort of kitchens they want and where the cupboards should be. It's great having a say in where things should go.

In the meantime they wait in the rotting tenement built before the war. Three-quarters of the building is empty and boarded up to stop vandals from smashing any more windows and getting at the pipes. Seven families remain in a state of siege. The other residents were offered maisonettes by the council and jumped at the chance. The rest, the members of the co-operative, stuck out for their own estate. It's a shame really. The tenement wasn't always the mess it is now. Somewhere along the line the authorities stopped maintaining it. Years ago they apparently had a proper community here; people shared what little they had. The hat went round when there was a death so that you could get your suit out of the pawn-shop. If a boy was starting work or a woman needed a shawl for the new baby, someone found a few ounces of wool or a pair of long trousers. There were parties for the kiddies, down there in the flooded courtyard - the end-of-the-war celebrations, the Coronation, that sort of thing. That was in the old days.

Nowadays Chris and Gwyneth keep out of the place as much as possible. They can't go out at night because of the children, but in the day Chris goes to the Sports Centre and Gwyneth helps out at the Wellington Street nursery. Little Robert goes to proper school but she takes the two little girls with her. It costs five pence a week, including milk and biscuits.

Gwyneth and her brothers and sisters were brought up in a children's home. Their mother died of cancer and as their father was a night-watchman he couldn't stay home to look after them. He lives down the road with his son Brian, and Gwyneth sees them regularly. One of her sisters travels the world and sends a postcard once a year, and another is married and has moved to Daventry. Her other sister, Val, lives round the corner with her husband David Murray and their children.

Chris has thought of leaving Liverpool. He's waiting to see if things improve, and now that he's working and there's the house to look forward to there isn't the urgency. Besides, he's a Liverpool football supporter and he would miss going to the matches. When you haven't got very much you need to feel you're part of something successful, unbeatable. He was heartbroken about the Brussels disaster. Afterwards, when the team played at Anfield the clergy were there to take prayers and something went wrong with the address-system. Those in the terraces couldn't hear a blessed word; they didn't know what was going on. That's why they began to sing. And of course the papers reported it as an act of disrespect and said that the Liverpool fans had once again demonstrated what hooligans they were, when the truth was that in singing 'You'll Never Walk Alone' they were paying their own tribute to the dead, chanting their own prayer.

David Murray, his brother-in-law, has been out of work for five years. Yesterday his wife Val went into hospital to have their third child. Ten months ago David was going to have a vasectomy but with the cut-backs they said he'd have to wait. They didn't intend to have another baby but now that he's here he's a blessing. A man's not less of a man because he's out of work. It's not that irresponsible. Love breaks down in the best of conditions and can survive the worst.

When asked how he managed to provide for his family, David said he didn't, at least not what he would call managing. But then, as he's not productive he supposes he's not entitled to much. Val gets £13.70 a week in family allowances and he gets a Giro cheque for £106.30 every fortnight and six milk-tokens. They live in a damp maisonette in Mornington Street which is slightly preferable to the tenement flat they lived in before. It's the landings that cause the trouble; people pee on them and throw out their rubbish.

If he could choose the sort of job he might do, he'd want to be a physical education instructor. He trains at the Sports Centre every day, the same one that Chris goes to, and he jogs as much as he can. There's nothing in the till at the Centre because if you're not working you get in free, and that's everybody. There isn't much chance of his getting the job he wants, or any other job for that matter.

'The reason you expect so little,' he said, 'is because you were born with so little and brought up with so little, and you get accustomed to it. You go to school and then they kick you out and tell you to fend for yourself, but how can you when there's nothing to go for. I owe Liverpool nothing; Liverpool owes me. The reason I don't leave here has nothing to do with Liverpool as a place, it is the people and the atmosphere. I live in one of the most notorious districts in England – Toxteth – and what it's notorious for is crime and vandalism and poor housing, but I've never known anywhere else. I suppose I'm conditioned – the family being all around sort of draws you, and they're always there to help you when it's needed. Just being called Daddy gives me a buzz. All we've really got is family.'

*

On the outside it's an ordinary little terraced house in a street running downhill to the river. They still have the air-raid shelter in the backyard. Inside it's a little palace. George Maclean has put in Tudor beams and knocked the two downstairs rooms into one. Rosie has hung brass kettles from the beams, copper pans and pewter mugs. There are more of them on the shelves above the fireplace alongside plates and jugs and rows of china figures. The family bring them back as presents every time they go on holiday. The fire-light is reflected in every dazzling surface, the kettles, the brass fender, the clock face, the ornate frame of the photograph of George in his army uniform and Rosie with a kiss-curl on her forehead.

George was born in a cellar-house in Hampton Street. His mother died of TB and he was brought up by his grandmother who had come over from Ireland and married a master carter who worked at the stables off Upper Parliament Street. He never knew his father. He lived with his sister Monica, his sister May, his Uncle Peter, Uncle Billy, Uncle Arthur, his grandmother and Uncle Billy's son Tommy, who got blown up in the war. He shared a bed with Tommy.

His grandmother respected people and taught him to do the same. She called everybody Sir, even if it was a tramp that came to the door. She wasn't servile or anything like that. He was brought up to be independent – you will not ask for that, what you haven't got you will not ask for. Rosie's mother was the same; she was a wonderful woman. She could fight like a man but she was good-hearted. They were great people in those days. You never went hungry. If there wasn't anything to eat at home you went down the street and if they had something, pease pudding or something in that line, they'd give you a plateful. You never asked, mind. There was Mrs Donnelly, Peter the Parrot, they called her, and she'd ask you in and sit you down and say, 'Have you had your dinner?' And you'd say, 'No, Mrs Donnelly,' and she'd give you the pudding. The Salvation Army used to come round with galvanised buckets of rice-pudding and soup. It cost twopence a bowl.

He was a terrible sagger at school. His grandma tried to get him into St Patrick's but it wasn't in the parish and he ended up at the Protestant school in St James's Road below the

46

cathedral. He used to take time off and go down to the cast-iron shore, where the Garden Festival site is now, and sit on the golf-links waiting for the tide to go out so that he could collect crabs.

He never knew anybody who was dirty in those days, or neglected: you could always keep yourself clean. Before you went to bed at night you held the oil lamp up to the walls – they were distempered blue or green – and the bugs fell out into the wick.

He and Rosie married when they were both seventeen. She'd always thought he was cheeky. Rosie wore a blue dress and a white hat. It was only over the road at St Malachie's – he was there at Mass this morning. They went to live with his sister May in Norfolk Street, on the top landing with a curtain across.

The first baby was born dead. It was a lovely baby, a lovely colour, and it was over nine pounds in weight. He went to the hospital and he said, 'What happened here?' and the doctor explained that they'd had to use instruments. So he said, 'How am I going to bury it?' He was signing on for juvenile dole at the time, basket-weaving in the morning and netball in the afternoon. If you didn't turn up they wouldn't give you the eighteen shillings a week. The doctor said he'd give him a note to take down to the Corporation Yard – the stink yard they called it – by Tate and Lyle's. They gave him the baby in a little box and he took it on the tram to Rosie's mother, to show it her. He put the box on the seat beside him on the tram, in case the electricity revived the baby, like Frankenstein, but it was no good. He knew it wouldn't, he was just being fanciful. After Rosie's Mam had seen it he went along to the Corporation Yard – there was a little sort of hatch at the side entrance – and he rang the bell. He had the letter from the hossie and he handed it over to the fellow in the hatch – he had the city bird on his hat – and he read it and he said, 'Oh yes, Mr Maclean', and he took the box and slammed the hatch shut. They burnt it in the incinerator.

They had twelve children after that. One of them, Anthony, was killed down the road. There used to be a railway line running along the dock road for the coal trucks and he got out and that was that. There's a photograph of him on the wall with his hand held up. He was holding a milk bottle when he had his photograph taken but they had that taken out later.

Rosie doesn't say much; she doesn't get the chance with George around. She sits there with little Bernard lolling against her knee. Opposite, on the wall above the fireplace, hangs a picture of the Virgin Mary with children kneeling at her feet. Now and then George looks across at Rosie for confirmation.

'I was never strict with the children, was I?' he asks.'Children bring themselves up. They come home from school and they play with each other. I never had any trouble with them, did I?'

'You were never there,' said Rosie, without rancour.

'No,' said George, 'I was on the long-distance lorries.' That was before he went into business for himself.

Their last boy, Michael, was a bit of a shock. He's eighteen now. Rosie went to the hossie with her daughter-in-law. She was having headaches with the blood pressure and Ann said she needed it looked at.

George was coming down the hill and he met Christopher coming up – he was working on the grain silo at the docks – and he shouted, 'Oh, Dad, oh dear, you're for it.'

George said, 'What are you on about?' When he got into the house Rosie wouldn't speak to him.

'The doctor examined me,' said Rosie, 'and he said I was pregnant. I said, I'm not. He said, you are. I said, I'm not. Me daughter-in-law ran out laughing.'

Rosie says that Michael has been spoilt, arriving so late and so unexpectedly. He's courting at the moment, in an on-off sort of way, though deep down he thinks the world of his girl. He too, like his older brothers, Tommy, George and

Bernard, is unemployed, but he's making the best of things.

They're all making the best of things in Liverpool. They didn't give much for Heseltine, they think even less of Mrs Thatcher and not many of them agree with the militants, and for all I know they scarcely give a thought to the technology that is making them redundant. The bad times are only temporary. Their optimism could be dismissed as an ostrich-like trait, were it not for the fact that contrary to popular belief the ostrich doesn't bury its head in the sand but simply ducks it behind a bush until the danger is passed. For over a century the Macleans, by some miracle of dogged perseverance, in spite of wars and demolitions, change and decay, have managed to stay put, ducking their heads and raising their families within sight of the river. Given a house and a job and a bit of a garden they would count themselves blessed. It might have been better for my father if he had thought the same; he had nothing to lose but his aitches.

2

The Coglans of Hastings

Graham Coglan's boat came in from the sea at four o'clock in the morning, ploughing the shingle with a noise like biscuits breaking. The crew jumped from the bows and prepared to winch the vessel out of the water. The boy ashore, who was no longer a boy, hauled on the rope which strained across his shoulder and staggered up the bank of shifting stones piled up by the tide. After each grating yard, as the bottom of the boat ground against the shingle, he slipped his rope and dipped into the darkness to lay another wooden skid for the keel to bite on. Later, running now and dragging behind him a makeshift sledge loaded with plastic bins, he ferried the catch to the fish-market higher up the beach.

The hawkers were already there, waiting for the bidding to begin. The auctioneer sat perched on a high stool beside the weighing machine. He was in his shirt sleeves and kept glancing to see what time it was by the gold watch he wore on his wrist. At his feet sat a perky white dog with a twisted tail.

The buyers wore anoraks and gum boots. Most of the younger fishermen were clad in blue overalls and plimsolls. They looked like farmers, which they were, if not of the land. An old man in a debonair yachting cap brought me a cup of tea. In his younger days he had been a sailor, not a fisherman. He told me that he was now seventy-five years of age and had been a boy ashore for the last fifteen. 'And I hope,' he said, 'that I shall be one for another fifty.' I assured him that he probably would, and indeed by the healthy look of him, ankles bare above his sodden sand-shoes, shoulders braced in his skimpy tee-shirt, it didn't seem all that unlikely.

The lights blazed under the metal shades and yet there

were shadows everywhere, pools of darkness where the dead fish flickered and the still living crabs and the ink-blue lobsters slithered in their wooden crates. In spite of the door open to the starlit beach, the shovelling of ice blocks which fell from the hods and skidded across the concrete floor puddled with sea-water, the air was warm, as if the sun was up.

Graham Coglan was not there. Either he had gone home or he was still down by the water seeing to the boat. It was the job of his boy ashore to attend to the selling of the fish, for which he received a quarter share of the night's takings.

When the bidding began the auctioneer hardly raised his voice above the skeetering of the plastic bins and the thump of the weighing machine. I took both him and the old sailor for working men and yet neither of them had an accent that I could detect.

The fish lay in batches, waiting to be costed. The plaice fell white sides upward, bouncing as they hit the metal basin of the scales. I thought them unremarkable creatures until I remembered the elaborate dance of their lower eye, which, once youth has passed, glides round their skull to the opposite side and fixes above the other. There was something else I had been told at school during one of those two interminable hours each week in which we were taught biology, something to do with silver eels and the Sargasso Sea, and now I wished I had listened to the migratory facts instead of paying attention to the alliteration, for just then they began bidding for eels, though these were not silver at all but a pinkish brown like an earthworm.

The old sailor was brushing up, sweeping the water out of the door. There was no offal or shards of fat. The fish were whole, inviolate, as if they had leapt into the nets of their own free will: sole, rock salmon, brill, mackerel, whelks half out of their shells, cod with gaping mouths, dabs with skins patterned like old carpet slippers, whitebait heaped in hills of silver. No wonder the story of the loaves and the fishes sounds so perfect. Two lumps of meat turning black in the sun and multiplied five thousand times would have made a blood-soaked miracle.

Outside the darkness was lifting. There were more boats coming in, lights rocking as they neared the water's edge. The morning star hung above the black sentry boxes of the tackle boxes on the foreshore. Down ran the piping ringed plovers and the oystercatchers, lifting into the air as the boats rode the swell and ground upon the shingle.

*

I had never been to Hastings before, and yet, on that first morning, having circled the stones of the castle and stood on the cliff-top to admire the view across the straits of Dover to Boulogne, I knew exactly in which direction to walk on the downward side. Indeed, arriving at a fork in the road I took a path which at first appeared to wander upwards, until, coming to a turning beside a ruined house, it plunged towards the commercial quarter of the New Town. For most people this wouldn't have had much significance, but my navigational sense is poor and I can get lost in streets I have known for twenty years. Even allowing for the fact that an expanse of sea cannot shift about and must lie roughly where it was last seen, it still didn't account for the peculiar feeling I had of familiarity with my surroundings. In particular with that blackened house whose back extension had fallen into rubble, exposing the remains of a mouldering staircase so delicately attached to the upper storeys that it resembled a mess of cobwebs hung above the gape of rotting floorboards through which the blackberry bushes sprang.

I kept climbing back down into the road to look at it from below, for it stood on a ridge and must at one time have had steps up to the front door. I had risen before dawn to go to the fish-market and possibly I was light-headed, but I couldn't rid myself of the impression that I had seen the house before, had stood on the stairs long ago. At one end, opposite the door, was an arched window, fortified with bars and edged with shards of coloured glass. The light filtering in from the invisible sky fell on the metallic glitter of a milk bottle top, and pictures went clicking through my head, one after the other – a soup-tureen set on a starched table-cloth, windows opening onto a terrace with a stone urn in the centre, a polished banister rail and a snake of Turkey carpet blanched by moonlight. It wasn't scarey; I saw no phantom figures, felt no shivers of foreboding. Nothing bad had happened in the house, except that it had been emptied and left to rot. I picked about in the undergrowth of the dead garden and unearthed only rags that rattled like old iron.

There was an elderly woman further along the road, watching me from her gate. I had to go and talk to her because old people get nervous when they see strangers loitering. I didn't want her to think that I was a burglar or a vandal, though there wasn't much scope for either one in that graveyard of a house.

'What is that place?' I asked, pointing.

'What place?' she said. For a moment I thought she meant that the house was visible only to me, and then an old man came up the side path carring a watering can and the woman said to him, 'What is that place, John?'

'What place?' he said, and turned to water his roses, though not before I had noticed the growth on the side of his face, coloured like a plum.

I walked on down the hill talking to myself, as one does on a warm day with no one about, thinking of old people and old houses and whether John minded that mark on his face, and whether he had been born with it or it had grown on later, like superfluous hair or corns, and what would he feel if he woke up one morning to find the mark gone and face skin whole again. And then it came to me, the reason why I had seemed to know the road and the house on the ridge.

I wrote a novel some years ago about a schoolmaster who

murdered his wife in 1871. He was an educated man without money or background and he lived through an industrial revolution which changed his world for ever. The dazzling and boundless commercial opportunism of Victorian England, its enormous prosperity and enterprise was founded on a mortgaged aristocracy, dependent on a gambling foreign commerce, and flourished through a home trade so morbidly competitive that a man's labour could be dispensed with as easily as falling off a log. For a time my hero achieved a measure of success as the headmaster of a small proprietary school in Stockwell, but already the old disciplines of Latin and Greek were being pushed aside in favour of the sciences and the tradesmen of North London were preparing to send their sons to the new boarding schools in the South. Soon, the headmaster too would be pushed aside, a victim of progress, that shifting tip beneath whose load it is always someone's turn to be buried.

My book was about cause and effect as much as anything else. The poor fellow was real, not invented, and particulars of his scholastic and criminal activities were well documented in the newspaper reports of the time and in records of his trial. Of his humdrum life, once his golden days at Trinity College had passed and he had married the desperate governess first glimpsed across a crowded drawing room in Dublin, little was known. As I was writing a novel rather than a biography I was under no necessity to stick to the facts; I could do what I liked with him. To show his sunny side I dispatched him and his wife on a holiday. Then as now, the seaside was popular. Simply dunking oneself in the waves was said to improve the health. The various Corporations provided bathing machines and marked off separate areas for the sexes. The women plopped into the water in voluminous dresses and drawers. The men wore nothing at all. It was even considered beneficial to drink the sea-water, and if the taste was too much to stomach it could be mixed with beer or port. I had thought of the Victorians as a puritanical breed, full of humbug and a sense of sin, unable to let themselves go – yet all that time they were disporting themselves in the sunshine, the men naked and the women half-seas over as they sailed like ducks on the briny.

I couldn't make up my mind where to send my schoolmaster for his vacation. I didn't want him in Blackpool because that was the North and he was a Londoner and why would he go all that way? I didn't think he should go to Brighton – Brighton was too flashy for him. So I chose Hastings. The name came out of my head like a number out of a hat. I say that, but then nothing is ever as random as it appears. In my opinion there's no such thing as imagination – in the sense that we have the power to form images of our own making – for unless we've already acquired images in the first place, from somewhere, how can we possibly summon them into existence, reformed or not? One can't be born with an imagination. It isn't the same thing at all as a pair of lungs or a toe or a blue eye. It must surely grow with us, built from lost conversations and forgotten events, dependent on impressions and sensations which fall through the mind like shooting stars; gathered from fuzzy remembrances of pictures in story books, of wallpaper patterns, fragments of nursery rhymes and Sunday school parables, whispers in the next room, footsteps in the dark, etc., etc. No matter – my schoolmaster went to Hastings.

I bought a guide book of the time and learnt that the Old Town lay in a valley between the East Cliff and Castle Hill. The fish-market was situated on the foreshore, down by the curious, tarred tackle lofts used by the fishermen to store their nets. The church of St Clements had a cannonball stuck in the masonry beside the belfry windows, fired during some long-forgotten bombardment. The corresponding ball on the other side was placed there from an eccentric desire of the vicar and the church wardens to make a balance in the design.

I sent my schoolmaster's wife meandering along the parade, pacing her steps to the oompah-pah of a German band. In the evening, attired in yellow silk, she sauntered beside the sea accompanied at a respectful distance by a troubadour dressed as a Spanish cavalier, strumming on a guitar. I wrote of her husband lying on the springy grass of the headland observing the behaviour of the gulls, and had him explore the ruins of the castle before clambering over the promontory to St Leonards.

They stayed in a boarding house high above the sea. One night, overcome with sunstroke, the wife went into a delirium. The schoolmaster sat on the stairs while the doctor attended to her. The front door had been left open – there were eight steps to the road below – and he could hear the crash of the waves on the distant shingle. He said out loud: 'Tired of the raging sea I'm getting sane, and my old scars are quite skin-whole again.' I took his words from a translation of some Greek tragedy, I forget which. The tragedy of a writer is that he can never remember, once his book is finished, where anything came from. It was meant to be a jolly holiday, but somehow it came out gloomy.

I made all of it up, including the picnic he took on the shore below the cliff where now the clockwork train of the perpendicular railway scuttles like a crab to the summit and bulges from the anus of the rock.

*

Clara Coglan was born in Hastings. Her father was a fisherman and his father before him, and he was drowned at sea. She left school at fourteen and worked in a laundry. The first time she set eyes on her husband was at a boxing match. She was courting a fighting man and Joe challenged him and knocked him out. Some months later she bumped into him on the parade and that was that. I ought to ask Joe about it. He'd tell me. They were married in 1935 on very little money. Two-pound-fifty a week didn't go very far with seven children to feed. They lived in those days in a little flat in the High Street, near the Jenny Lind pub which her son Roy has recently bought, and now she and Joe are both over seventy and they have a council house all to themselves. Things used to be so hard, and now it's so much better you can hardly believe it. It doesn't seem possible.

We were having lunch together at the Blue Dolphin cafe on the front. The door was open and I could see a solitary little boy in a sun-hat travelling in a painted carriage along the kiddies' railway. Behind him the wind-breakers and the empty deck-chairs ballooned in the breeze.

The fish and chips on our plates were the best I had ever tasted and yet we both knew it was a bit of a waste. I was ravenous from my dawn visit to the market and all that walking about the headland, and perhaps Clara was hungry too, but it's not easy conducting a personal conversation with a stranger when you're jammed elbow to elbow and you have to keep passing the vinegar and the salt, and shortly she put down her fork and stopped eating altogether. 'You carry on,' she said. 'Don't mind me.'

I asked her what she did in Hastings, by way of amusement. 'Not a lot,' she said, and gave me an old-fashioned look. She wasn't one for pubs or anything like that. In fact not a mixer at all. She kept herself to herself.

'A home bird,' I said.

'Something like that,' she replied, though once a year she and Joe went up North to visit his younger brother. Not that she ever felt well up there. The North didn't agree with her. Some of the people were charming, but they had different ways – for instance, the chips were always too greasy.

It wasn't such a slight thing to pick on. She could hardly help noticing the way I shovelled the food into my mouth. I was taken aback by the word charming. Nobody up North would use such an adjective.

Nor was she political. She voted, of course, but only after

Joe had made up his mind where to put his cross. Not that there was ever any doubt about where that would be. Joe was a northerner, the son of a miner from Durham. As a boy he had worked down the pit and after the strike of 1926 they wouldn't take him back and he came down South. There was a terrible feeling against the miners after the strike. People thought that in withholding their labour like that they had worsened everybody's lives. Still, he stayed put. He did all sorts of jobs, anything he could turn his hand to. He worked as a foreman building the jetties at Shoreham and along the Thames Valley – and then he became a fisherman. He had to retire early because of his chest.

She wouldn't like to repeat what he thought of Mrs Thatcher. Dear me, no. Joe was a great man for discussing politics, or anything else for that matter. All sorts of things made him mad. 'You want to talk to him about it,' she said. 'He'll put you right.' He was in hospital again with his lungs. Josie, their daughter, was a cleaner at the same hospital. She was on the early morning shift and I could talk to both of them while I was at it. I'd get far more out of Joe.

'What sort of things make him mad?' I persisted, and again she gave me that look, raising her eyebrows as if to say what doesn't he get mad about. Then I knew the way it was, and how it had been for her. No matter how long it had been since Joe had left his roots he still retained his northern belligerence, his argumentative temperament born of hard times and different customs, and he would go on being riled by the soft-spoken southerners and their softer deprivations until the seas froze over.

Clara was like Rosie and yet she wasn't. Life had got the boot in in a different manner. It wasn't that she was hiding anything or showing a natural reluctance to bare her soul to somebody she didn't know; it was more that she didn't see what good it would do talking about it.

I left her in peace and went down on to the beach to meet her son Roy. He was mending his nets. The foreshore is the fishermen's workshop, littered with discarded machinery and bales of cable, lengths of rope and plastic drums, eroded anchors, chains, tarpaulins, old lobster pots and refuse from the sea. Even when the weather is bad and he can't go out in his boat, a fisherman never twiddles his thumbs. A vessel is an expensive investment and has to be properly maintained. Its owner has to be a bit of an engineer, an electrician, a carpenter. And then he has his nets to see to, stringing them up between two posts and plucking on them as though fingering a limp harp, pulling away the sea-wrack which flutters from every knot, repairing the threads with a metal wedge shaped like a shoehorn. The beach may look a mess to the uninitiated eye but every piece of junk is there for a purpose and could come in handy at any moment. Besides, this part of the shore belongs to the fishermen by deed, and all those letters of complaint written from townsfolk to the council are so much ink on the wind.

Roy wanted to go to sea right from the start. As a child he was never off the beach. The flat they lived in was so small that he and his brother Graham were glad to be out of it. And when they were a bit older they could earn money down here – helping with the catch, swilling out, greasing, running errands. They gave every penny to Mother because she had a hard time trying to make ends meet.

At fifteen he left school to work in a lampshade factory. He met his wife Barbara there. Her mother came from Somerset and her father was a builder in Hastings. She was one of nine children. Before she took over the pub she did auxiliary nursing, looking after handicapped children. She worked the night shifts so as not to neglect her own. He helps Barbara behind the bar on a Saturday and Sunday – weekdays he's out in the boat.

He quit the factory to become a bricklayer. The old fellow, Joe, wouldn't hear of him going to sea. He said he had to learn a trade, and when the old fellow told you to do something you did it. Joe was prejudiced against the fishing;

in the fifties, when he was at sea, half the industry withered away and it hadn't really recovered since. The waters had got rich during the war and they were over-fished afterwards because there were no controls.

When he was twenty-two and had served his time, he and Graham set up in the building business for themselves. They didn't like it. They used to meet in a cafe at six o'clock in the morning before work, a whole gang of them, and they'd sit looking out of the door at the lights winking in the straits and they'd think what fools they were, going off to Peacehaven to build houses when they could be out there in the dark, fishing.

All the same, he stuck it out, they both did, and fifteen years later they had enough money saved to buy a fish-shop between them and a boat each. A new boat could set you back fifty thousand pounds, and gear wasn't cheap either. That mound of net over there might look like a lump of old flotsam but it was worth six hundred pounds or more. You couldn't leave the old cotton nets out like that but the nylon ones will stand anything, except sunshine. Once the economics of fishing had been taken into consideration – if the weather was bad you could be laid up ashore for weeks on end – the freedom, the knowledge that you were your own man and nobody could tell you what to do was beyond calculation. Fishermen had to be individualistic, independent. They dealt with elemental forces and they were on their own. They could be the best of friends on shore but if you were out at sea and trouble blew up it was every man for himself.

The industry was in decline, like most things, and while it could last him out, his son Darren, who had been at sea for eighteen months, might well outlive it. And he hadn't a trade to fall back on. Even if the fishing did give out before he himself was old enough to retire, he'd find another job. He'd never been on the dole in his life and wherever he lived he'd always find employment. If he had been unfortunate enough to have been born up North, and things were like they were, he'd shift himself quick as a flash, just as the old fellow had done. There wouldn't be any of that business about not wanting to leave your family or your home. Not that he'd like to move. The Old Town community was a close one – working down on the shore, watching the tides, discussing the weather, the catches – and possibly he was insulated from the way the rest of the country lived, the North in particular. He went up there twice over twenty years ago and he's not in a hurry to repeat the journey. His daughter Natalia was married to a chap from Liverpool who moved here because he was unemployed. He found the South an eye-opener. If he could get a job up there he'd go back tomorrow. He thinks southern women are too independent, too bossy. In Liverpool it's taken for granted that men should go out drinking on their own. Here, the women put their foot down. And he thinks the wages are lower in the South than in the North and the only way you can earn decent money is to work ten hours a day, and being young he's not into that. The only good thing about Hastings, he says, is that he can walk home from the pub without being hit over the head. His brother was killed outside a club in Liverpool.

You don't find people down here going on about where they come from. The way northerners talk you'd think they were a separate race and had a monopoly on hard times. He and Graham had never gone short of food as children but they'd never had any pants or vests or socks or luxury items of that sort. And they'd washed in a tin bath in front of the fire. Poverty wasn't a prerogative of the North. It was all very well for Scargill to demand that things should remain the same, whatever the economic realities, but what had that to do with facts. Facts demonstrated that steel and coal were done with, and it was no use moaning over it. All that sentimental nonsense about communities – the way they carried on you'd think coal-mining and shipbuilding had existed for their benefit. Maggie had the right idea. She was doing a good job, spelling it out right down the line.

*

I was walking up the High Street later that afternoon when an object in the window of an antique shop caught my attention. It was made of polished wood and shaped like a plump pin-cushion. It was sat on top of a lidded coal scuttle and I couldn't think what it might be. I went inside to make enquiries and the woman said an old man had brought it into the shop six months ago hoping it might be worth something. He had asked five pounds for it but I could have it for three. She said it was a measurer, the sort used on building sites at the beginning of the century. It still worked. She tugged on the little brass flap at the top and jerked out a metal tape. 'Not centimetres, of course,' she said, 'but I don't suppose you'll be using it.' I insisted on giving her five pounds, which was silly of me because I don't expect she handed on the extra to the old man. When I was in the road I pulled the tape out again and it dangled for yards. I couldn't shove it back in and I had to trail it behind me, waggling stiffly in the breeze and making a twanging noise. It had seemed a purchase made on impulse but was in fact a compulsive act of selection, if unconscious, for although I had felt nothing beyond a mild curiosity when I had spotted it in the window, the moment I held it in my hand I had known it had something to do with the schoolmaster and my choice of his holiday town.

When I was growing up in Formby by the sea there was a lady called Mrs Woodward in our village who took me to a concert at the Floral Hall in Southport to hear Paderewski play. She was well over seventy and her husband had been a music critic on a Liverpool newspaper. She was obviously educated, marrying a man like that, and what my mother called well bred – for instance she drank coffee after her meal instead of tea. I had met her in Derbyshire's sweetie shop in the village when choosing library books for my mother and she took a fancy to me. I must have been showing off, sneering at the romantic fiction all about doctors and nurses which my mother preferred and which I read almost as fast as she did, and pretending that I only read serious novels. She asked me to tea several times and I was disappointed to find that she lived in a bungalow and put doyleys under the cake-stand. On one of those occasions I met a lady called Mrs Criddle whose husband was something big in sugar and practically owned Tate and Lyle. She was old too and her coat had moth holes in it. Then Mrs Woodward telephoned my mother and asked if she could take me to a concert. My mother was thrilled. She made me wear her fox fur – I was thirteen at the time – and a pair of leather gloves. There was a handbag to match with nothing in it save a two-shilling piece with which to buy a programme. I wasn't very keen on music, not in real life. Often I listened in the dark to the wireless with my father, but that was different. I used to like the coughing at the beginning. I'd certainly never been to an actual concert and I was surprised at how much I enjoyed it, although I didn't hear any of the music beyond the opening bars; the minute the piano really got going, trilling up and down like raindrops, I went into daydreams and only came out of them when I heard the clapping at the very end. After it was over Mrs Woodward took me backstage to a dark little dressing-room with a gas lamp on the wall and I shook hands with Paderewski. He was a small man with a lot of mad white hair and he said he thought I had some kind of specialness – I remember the exact word – but it was only because I was looking at him in a very intense way, out of politeness. My mother never got over it, me shaking hands with a famous pianist, though she too didn't know him from Adam.

Some months later Mrs Woodward died, and afterwards Mrs Criddle telephoned my mother and said could I go to tea with her. 'Whatever have you been saying to these ladies?' demanded my mother, but secretly she was pleased.

The Criddles lived over the railway line in Wicks Lane in a wonderful house covered in dust, gloomy and full of books and sepia photographs of men with staring eyes under peaked caps. I don't think Mrs Criddle would have known a doyley if she had fallen over one. The house was always full of people, some of whom must have come on trains from somewhere strange because they all looked like tramps and spoke like teachers and called each other comrade. Even the ones that spoke with provincial accents talked as if they never had their noses out of a book. One time there was a young man lying on the sofa with bandages round his chest. He was a 'Bevin boy', Mr Criddle said, and he had been crushed against the coal face by a truck. The 'Bevin boy' described the incident. One moment he had been standing there with his pick and then he had heard that noise, that whooshing noise, and too late turned to see the black truck rushing for his heart.

Every week we put sixpence into the kitty to save up to buy tickets to go to a play at the end of the year. It was being written by the Criddles' youngest son and it was called *The Man with a Plan*. It would be put on at a proper theatre. My mother had already decided that I should go on the stage so she was as pleased as punch.

Mrs Criddle lent me books to take home. My father was in sympathy with the titles. They were all left-wing book choices dealing with the Russian Revolution and the Socialist Movement and he said he approved. I did a pen-and-ink drawing of Marshal Stalin and he pinned it up on the wall under the Swansea Tin-Plate Company's calendar. My brother called him Joe after that. It was out of one of Mrs Criddle's books that I tore the photograph of Rasputin.

I visited the house in Wicks Lane for almost a year, until Paul Robeson came to Liverpool. It was winter and I went with the Criddles and the comrades to a meeting outside St George's Hall. I don't remember what the meeting was about and I don't know why Robeson was there, but I won't forget him singing 'Tote that barge and lift that bale'. Mrs Criddle was crying. And then suddenly the police arrived and I got hit on the shoulder with a truncheon. I had hoped I could lie down on the Criddles' sofa and be fussed over as a casualty of the capitalist state, but I only had a small bruise to show for it and they made me go straight home. When he heard what had happened my father said it was a damned disgrace, running round Liverpool with a bunch of blasted anarchists. At the mention of the police all his principles went out of the window and he never let me go to the Criddles' again. But during one of those evenings sitting round the fire discussing the plight of the working man, Mrs Criddle had jumped up to find a book she wanted to show me. She couldn't locate it but it was by a man called Robert Tressell who had written of Hastings and the building trade and the terrible conditions existing at the time. He died in Liverpool Infirmary and his book wasn't published for years. He hadn't mentioned the fishing or the sea and he called his town by a different name, but it was Hastings all right.

*

Graham and Janet Coglan bought their house three years ago, high above the sea with gardens front and back, rock-terraced down the hillside. Inside there's a hearth big enough for log fires, and an open staircase. It's a stylish and comfortable house, the sort featured in gracious living magazines, though without the obligatory plants and coffee-tables. Outside on the patio there's a barbecue stand. Someone is fond of garden gnomes. A dozen or more decorate the rockeries, grinning alongside a stone hedgehog and a Disneyland toadstool full of wicked elves.

Graham fishes for twelve to fifteen hours a day. He says

that compared with the trawlers up North – the few that are
left – who go out for three weeks at a time, he's playing at
the game. He loves the sea; sometimes he can't sleep at night
for looking forward to the day's work. All he ever thought
about when he was on the building was of the day when he
would have his own boat, be his own man. He didn't have to
learn fishing; it was always part of his life. As a boy he was
either down on the beach helping out, or off in a rowing boat
with Roy, dangling a line over the side. Perhaps it was in his
blood. On his mother's side the fishing goes back
generations. There are drawbacks, of course; constant
checks on over-fishing, controls, fluctuations in the market –
the EEC has put the lid on the coffin – the weather, but then
the building trade was dependent on the weather too.
Fishing isn't subsidised like farming, though if you were laid
up ashore for over a certain length of time you could claim
the dole. Not that he ever has or ever would. They had a
hard time as youngsters and perhaps that has made him
more of a fighter, more determined than most to rely on
himself and provide a better life for his children. If a man's
in business for himself he can give employment to his
family. His sister Val's son crews for him, and his son
Lawrence works a boat with Roy's lad, Darren. When they
had the fish shop in the High Street they all lent a hand. A
factory worker can't do that for his family. All his brothers
and sisters have done well for themselves. The girls, Val and
Rosie, Pam and Pauline, are married to good husbands, and
they're all in employment. Josie works as an orderly at the
same hospital in which the old fellow is coughing up the coal
dust. She's worried at the moment about her job, on account
of the cut backs in the health service. It's a dilemma for her
really; she likes what Mrs Thatcher stands for and yet she
might be put out of work.

Young Peter is a plasterer. He used to be in the fishing
trade but he couldn't earn enough to support his wife,
Sandra, and their three children – you don't if you're not the

master of the boat – and so he went into the building trade. He's buying his own house now. He's the gypsy of the family; he keeps polecats at the end of his garden and takes them rabbiting up on the downs. He's a countryman, not the sort who cultivates the land but one who knows how to live off it. His kind go way back in time. He can tell you where the hares are running and how to snare and poach and stalk. Why, when William the Conqueror landed, someone like Peter was down there waiting for him, ready to find him a horse or show him where to pitch the tents.

None of the family had done well at school. A man required particular skills to know how to fish the sea – a mixture of intuition and commonsense, an awareness of currents and tides and the movement of the stars – and that sort of thing wasn't learnt at school.

Graham is reasonably contented with his life. These last few years he's been able to afford a higher standard of living. Before that the money went on different priorities: the shop, gear for the boat, the children. Now they can go out for the odd evening meal in a restaurant, enjoy a few bottles of wine at home with friends. It wasn't that they couldn't run to a glass of wine a year or so back, more that they had just never got round to the habit. It's a question of a changing life-style.

It wouldn't be the same for him if he fished up North. He stayed at his auntie's once and he was left with an impression of bleakness and desolation. There was a long back garden with a toilet at the end. It was medieval.

His wife Janet was born in Hastings in better circumstances. Her mother and father only had the two children, herself and her brother. Her mother Renée is an influence in her life. Renée didn't approve of Graham at first. She thought that bricklaying was an irregular occupation. She herself had worked for the Provident Hire Purchase Company and had dealt with too many self-employed customers defaulting on their payments. She didn't want

Janet living a hand-to-mouth existence. When she and
Graham were first married, Janet used to pretend that
Graham was employed in one place. She didn't let on that he
was moving from site to site because her mother would have
worried. Renée, now widowed, lives in a flat above an estate
agents' office at the top end of the town. She's handsome
and capable and every day she plays bowls with her partner,
Frank, up on the green on the Downs. In the evening she
and Frank go ballroom dancing, dressed up to the nines,
fitter than when they were young. She was a Tiller Girl
before she was married.

Janet has taken in lodgers – foreign students from the
English language schools – on and off for the last twenty
years, and when they had the fish shop she served in it from
five in the morning until seven o'clock at night. Since then
she hasn't worked, not in that sense of the word. She takes
care of the house and the garden and provides meals for
Graham and Lawrence and the boy from Switzerland who is
their current lodger.

She gives more thought to the political situation than
Graham does. Last time round she made him go out and
exercise his right to vote – before that he hadn't bothered.
Next time it will be more difficult to know who to vote for.
There are good points to Mrs Thatcher, the values she stands
for, the fact that she's a woman, but against that there are
the unemployment figures, the giving away of 37 per cent of
the fishing industry, the judges' pay rise.

They see on television how it is up North and it's hard to
take in, until she remembers the winter of 1963 when
Graham had been laid off bricklaying because of the severe
weather and she had found a job in a factory. Graham was
going out rabbiting and selling them for two shillings each.
He was shovelling snow – anything he could lay a hand to.
She hadn't been at the factory for more than a few weeks
when she went down with the flu; she was really ill and
couldn't go on. And then Graham came home with a

one-and-sixpenny bottle of Lucozade and she burst into tears because they couldn't afford it. Those were bad times and sometimes she thinks of them when she's out there in the sunshine gardening among the painted gnomes.

*

I had gone back to that ruined house which drew me like a magnet and was standing in the road looking up at it when a dog turned the corner. Attracted by a rustling in the bushes above, a bird perhaps or a field mouse, it leapt for the ridge and failing to gain a toe-hold dropped back into the road and fell awkwardly on to its haunches. Righting itself and shaking its back leg it limped away round the corner.

There are times when we suddenly find relevant hitherto unrelated statements made either in books or within colloquial expressions. For instance – 'something nasty in the woodshed', 'all my eye and Betty Martin', though those perhaps are easy examples, the one a salacious happening, the other to do with incredulity. But what of those lines of Hazlitt, which I had read over and over when young simply because it was pleasurable in adolescence to feel melancholy, never doubting for one moment that experience was particular rather than universal: *Man is the only animal that laughs and weeps; for he is the only animal that is struck by the difference between what things are and the way they might have been.* I repeated the words to myself with closed eyes, trying to work out whether I was thinking in words or images, and if the meaning of either one was comprehensible without the other. *Man is the only animal* was difficult, for the thought was accompanied by a picture of a dog walking upright, or rather a series of upright dogs. And there was a further confusion in the phrase *what might have been*, for now I saw a back-cloth wood and Margaret in *Dear Brutus* looking for her lost Daddy in the moonlight.

I fell to thinking of North and South – I was leaving

Hastings in the morning to travel to Barnsley – and the very juxtaposition of words put up pictures with labels – dark satanic mills, the swan of Avon. It is a softer life down here in the South, no question of that. There's not the same preoccupation with location or class. Not many round here thump their chests and talk of their regional roots, or hark back to a nostalgic past when everyone lived on bread and dripping. They're not given to self-analysis, and perhaps the so-called southern reserve is not so much a matter of unfriendliness as a detached complacency born of comparative affluence. Nothing divides a people more than riches, whether it be money in the bank or a quality of life, and it could be that the unification of a nation is dependent on collective hardship.

An hour later, standing on the headland to take a last look at the sun drowning in the water, I tried saying Hastings out loud, but neither the shades of my schoolmaster nor the ragged trousered philanthropists formed in my mind, and all I saw was what was there to be seen, a postcard view of sands and sea.

3

The Brittons of Barnsley

Time was when you could go on an outing to a town barely thirty miles distant from your own and it was like visiting another country. The shops sold different goods and the names painted above the doors were unfamiliar. You could go to Preston for Swedish furniture – though God knows why it had ended up there to Southport for a frock from the Bon Marché, to Ormskirk for bedding plants, to Pot Williams in Warrington for cups and saucers. Even the people seemed foreign, and the air was so heady and strange that you came back giddy, as if drugged, and yawned for days. Now, no matter how far you travel you arrive at the same place – whether in Clapham or Southampton, Nottingham or Weston-super-Mare, the carrier bags from the identical chain stores bowl in the wind along the paved wastes of the identical precincts.

Barnsley was once a quaint little town with a few dignified civic buildings and a market place going back to the twelfth century. Sheffield had steel and Leeds had Montague Burton's. Barnsley had coal. It was ringed with mining villages, a pit at the top end and another at the bottom, and the slag heaps rose in a wild landscape that climbed to the wildest of moors. The market has since gone and so has the coal, and the oldest building I saw on my first morning – I didn't count the Town Hall which was built in 1933 – was a Co-op down a side street, empty and unused but with a curious industrial chimney tacked on to the back, puffing steam.

For the rest, the people seemed the same as anywhere else, neither poorer nor more cussed than the newspapers would have us believe, and the young girls who queued at the pie shop for their dinner rolls were dressed – as young girls dress all over the North of England whatever the weather –

in mini-skirts and high-heeled shoes.

Rita and Geoff Britton live in a village outside Barnsley, though both have business premises in the town. Geoff is an accountant and Rita owns the dress shop, 'Pollyanna'. They had asked me to dinner, a celebratory occasion for the twenty-fifth wedding anniversary of old friends, John and Jill, who had come from the South for the weekend. We toasted them in champagne, and Rita said she wasn't going to shout aloud how long she and Geoff had been married because it might be embarrassing for the children – they have three sons at boarding school in Wakefield – at any road, she had held out for quite a while. Then suddenly she put down her glass and said, 'It's our fourth anniversary,' and glanced across at Geoff.

'This will cheer us up,' muttered Geoff.

'Four years ago to the day,' Rita said, 'I found out that I had cancer. After I'd had the operation Jill came to see me and the funny thing was that Jill looked awful. She really did.'

'It's true,' said Jill. 'I'd gone to sympathise with her and all she went on about was how ill I looked.'

'Four years ago to the day,' Rita said, 'since I found out what life really was.'

'Water under the mill,' said Geoff.

The house was lovely; log fires in the stone hearths, dogs in the kitchen, settles and sideboards, stout walls and a polished oak staircase you could break your neck on. My Uncle Len had a house that was meant to be like this, though his was of red brick and built in the years before the war, and my mother thought it wonderful even if it was filled with old furniture. In my uncle's lounge, while doing my imitation of Colonel Chinstrap, I had once knocked my cousin Hilary off the arm of her chair and she'd fallen into the glass-fronted bookcase and cut her head open. She ran round the room with a piece of glass sticking up out of her hair like a Spanish comb, and I thought I'd killed her and that she was running as chickens do when they're already dead. My

Uncle Len was furious about the bookcase.

Years later I had my wedding reception at his house because it was handy for the church. I had become a Catholic in Dundee while I was working at the repertory company there, and neither my parents nor my bridegroom cared to be seen going in or out of a Catholic church and picked one miles away from either Formby or Liverpool. I wanted to put wild flowers in my hair but my mother said I had made enough of a show of them as it was and made me wear a hat instead. She was dressed up in bright red like a cardinal, and my father complained that he had never known such a palaver in all his days, all that bobbing up and down during the service as though a mass outbreak of St Vitus's dance had swept the pews. He said he felt worn out. My mother was annoyed that it couldn't be a long dress affair. It would have been if she'd had her way, only the groom outwitted her and chose a friend with a humped back for his best man and we couldn't hire a jacket to fit him.

Rita said that she wasn't at all sure she approved of the marriage contract. She had lived as a child with her mother and grandmother. All the menfolk in the family had gone away and it was a matriarchal society. Born during the war, she didn't remember her father until it was over. Her mother had been blackleading the fireplace and a neighbour had scuttled in and said, 'I've just seen your Arthur down the road at the bus station', and her mother ran off – it was but a cock-stride down the road – and there was her husband in his uniform with a kitbag over his shoulder, standing there after all those years. She forgot herself and ran to him, holding out her arms. 'Hey up,' he said. 'Everybody's looking at us.'

After that Rita and her mother and father went to live in a council house. It was terribly cold in that house in the winter and it was lovely going back to her grandmother's every Friday to bathe in a tin tub in front of the fire.

Geoff said his father hadn't been in the war because he was working in the foundry. And he'd had his leg burnt off anyway.

'Burnt off?' I said.

'His brain worked better afterwards,' said Geoff.

It was not so much a matter of northern grit as the strength derived from belonging to a working community, a community which after all those struggling years was now dying, if not dead.

Rita said that both her mother and her grandmother had been as bright as buttons, even if uneducated, and she can't ever remember thinking that anything was beyond her own capabilities. They mightn't have told her much about opera or ballet or the benefits of higher education, but she did know that she was a person in her own right. She left school at fifteen and went first into a sewing factory and then into a paper-mill. The mill was a cut above an ordinary job and you could only get taken on if you had connections, rather like an upper-crust but impoverished family trying to get their lad into the public school his father had gone to before him. Her mother had worked there and an aunt and an uncle and two cousins. She stayed for eight years, sorting paper by hand and counting it into reams.

Twenty years ago she decided to set up the first boutique in Barnsley. The fashion industry had started to boom and it was easy to jump into that sort of thing in the sixties. She opened her first 'Pollyanna' shop in the Shambles at a rent of £4 a week. But she was changing all the time, reading more and thinking more, and in the end she wanted to sell proper clothes with designer labels, not because it was more up-market or anything like that but because she wanted to stock the very best. Skill and training and brains went into the making of those sort of clothes, as well as the best materials and workmanship, and that's why they cost so much more than the cheap copies churned out in inferior cloth by the chain stores. A skirt or a jumper made by one of the Italian houses or by Jean Muir might cost £275, but what of it? Nobody would think twice of spending £2000 on a car or a holiday. Jean Muir always refers to herself as a dressmaker, and it's true, and what she makes is as lasting and beautiful as a piece of craftsman-made furniture or china. It's something to do with the line of the clothes as much as the cloth. The cheap stuff goes out of fashion almost as soon as it's bought and falls apart at the cleaners. 'I know it sounds pretentious,' she said, 'but it saddens me the way young girls are being exploited. I mean the way they're programmed into buying mini-skirts and skimpy tops just so it will attract the men.'

'It will attract the men all right,' said Geoff.

'But all that rubbish comes from Taiwan,' protested Rita. 'And the poor beggars making it get nothing but a bowl of rice for their trouble. Why can't the youngsters wait a bit and save up for something decent which will last? They pay eight pounds fifty one week for a red skirt, and eight pounds fifty the next for another one in blue, and nine pounds ninety-nine for a rag of a blouse with its buttons already coming loose.'

'That's twenty-six quid, ninety-nine pence,' said Geoff, every inch the accountant.

Still, we all knew what Rita meant, for we were all of the generation who had been brought up to believe that decent clothes were a mark of respectability.

My mother didn't think it was nice to buy off the peg, not even my school uniform. Miss Smith in Ainsdale made my gym slips. My mother didn't ask my Auntie Margo to do the dressmaking because she said all Margo's patterns came out of the ark, and besides, most of her dress materials had come from Blacker's bomb damage sale after it was burnt out during the May blitz. It was true that sometimes my Auntie Margo looked like a woman gutted by fire, the glitter in her over-emphatic eyes matching the glittering sequins scattered in a trail of sparks across the scorch marks of her Sunday cocktail frock.

Miss Smith was very short in stature and had to stand on tiptoe when she chalked my arm holes. Something tragic had happened to her when young, after which she had never grown again. Her father had been a lavender-cart man – collecting the muck from the cesspits of the cottages down by the shore – and Miss Smith in childhood had been kicked by his horse, though some said it was her father who had done the kicking. Her lips clamped on a row of pins, trembled on a level with the top button of my liberty bodice, and I was always leaning backwards as we stood there chin to chest as if waiting for some dance-tune to begin. She was shy and retiring unless she was actually wielding her tape measure or applying her bit of chalk. 'Two pleats,' she'd say, 'would look better than one.' And once, 'Might I suggest a small pocket at the side, for a handkerchief?' We didn't run to handkerchiefs in our family but my mother was taken with the idea. If she criticised Miss Smith, mentioned that the hem was a little crooked or the waist a fraction too high, Miss Smith stood with her hands clenched at her sides, a look of resignation on her face, as though expecting another kick. But for shy Miss Smith and her innovatory pocket I would never have been expelled from school.

My mother went to a tailor to be fitted for her costumes, as did my father for his suits. They were made to last a lifetime, and they did, and my father had an overcoat of such superior cloth that whenever he wore it he almost sank to his knees under its weight.

*

Geoff said he had been influenced more by his Dad than his mother. As a lad he was always down at the foundry with his father. The only reason he took up accountancy was because he was no good at casting and his Dad didn't want him to go down the pit. When he was doing his articles he developed serious eye trouble and nearly went blind. For a time he had to use a white stick. He worked in London for almost two years and he was amazed at how London businessmen blabbed; up here they played their cards close to their chests.

Most of his clients live in the Barnsley area. Yesterday, for instance, he had spent most of the morning at Shotties Island with the owners of a scrap-metal yard. One of the partners had started out as a miner. From the gates there was a view of Royston drift mine, its burner stack blowing a red flame, its chimney belting out smoke. That sort of pollution was taken for granted, and yet while he was there some bugger came in to complain about the rubber burning in the yard. It was daft. The yard takes in ninety per cent of the country's old buses and reduces them to small bundles in twenty minutes flat. The trick is to know which bits are the most valuable.

'You'd like it down there,' he said. 'They've got a great jagged pile of metal like something ready for the Tate Gallery. There's combustion engines and gear-boxes, old seats and stairways. It's quite artistic – red buses for London, orange for Wales, Tyne and Wear is yellow, and green for Liverpool. There's one that got burnt out in the riots. And they've all got adverts on the side, so you can date them if you've a mind to. Evita, Fly Delta to the USA, It's Got to be Gordon's, Torvil and Dean, and a Nestlés van all tangled up with dandelions and bindweed. It's a very successful business, that scrap yard.'

Accountancy, he said, wasn't just about money, it was knowing which people could win through. Usually when a business went wrong it was the fault of the boss not the business. He's not in favour of the government giving subsidies just because certain parts of the country are in trouble. They handed out tax incentives and reduced rates, and then what happened? The other manufacturers, who weren't on subsidies, put up their prices. They couldn't compete otherwise, and then they priced themselves out of business. Next, the government cut the subsidies to the other lot and they went down the drain too. It was bloody ridiculous. 'There's an old Chinese proverb,' he said. 'Give a man a fish and you give him a meal for the day. Teach him to fish and you feed him for a lifetime.'

I told him I'd met a family in Hastings whose father had been a miner in the strike of 1926. Geoff said his grandfather had lived through that and in the end it had killed him. I should talk to his father about it. He'd tell me the difference between that strike and this last one.

'I can't forgive Scargill,' said Rita.

'How can anybody talk of being in support of the strike,' Geoff said, 'if they're not prepared to burn coal in their grate?'

'He should never have started it unless he knew he could win,' said Rita. 'You'd think he was working for the government the harm he's done to Barnsley. It's split us all down the middle and we won't ever be the same again.'

*

On Sunday I went to the Moulder's Arms to listen to the Shepley Brass Band. Outside in the breezy sunlight they were racing pigeons and exercising their greyhounds. I was sat at a table with John and Margaret Warburton, trying to get John to talk about his job as an electrician on the coal face at the new colliery, but both he and Margaret were distracted because their son Robert was about to give a cornet solo. He performed it very well and we clapped him heartily at the finish. He's a surface-worker at the mine and his parents are worried that he hasn't got a future. They didn't particularly want him to go down the pit, but what else was there for him? When he left school they'd already begun to clamp down on recruitment, and but for the fact that John had put his name down years back he wouldn't have got in. He was underground at first and then he developed bronchial asthma. There was talk that the pit he's at had another five years of life, and they've just spent forty million pounds sinking a new shaft, but now there's rumours that it could close after all. If that happened then Barnsley was done for. It would become a ghost town.

John is Rita's cousin. 'When we were little,' he said, 'we were like brother and sister. We don't see so much of each other now. We were more on a level then. Well, she's got her business and we've got our work and there isn't the closeness any more. It's sad really when you look back. We were happier then, even if we hadn't got as much.'

He was reluctant to discuss the strike. There were things that had happened, on both sides, which disgusted him. He hates his job now. The atmosphere's all wrong because people are frightened they'll lose their places and nobody's ever told what the situation really is. He broke the strike for one day, when he was desperate. He went back out the next. He didn't feel guilty about going back, and Margaret supported him, but afterwards men he had known all his life wouldn't speak to him. He's put in for voluntary redundancy. He's not saying that before the strike he loved his work or anything daft like that, just that it's no longer the same. He thinks the miners were used to do other people's dirty political washing.

Margaret works at S.R. Gents clothing manufacturers, printing labels. When the strike was on she and John swopped roles. He became a great cook and she was astonished. All the same it was a relief when the strike ended. 'I don't mind telling you,' she said, 'we were getting to the edge. I had my week's pay to come and £40 left in the savings bank. Mind you, we were better off than most. Some got very heavily into debt; it was terrible for them. Quite a few of the families didn't survive, marriage-wise that is.' She's not saying that it brought her and John closer, because they've always been close and it's a very happy marriage, and it was awful knowing how helpless he felt, sitting at home all day sorting out his shell-collection and worrying about Robert and the future.

I thought that Margaret looked like Louise Brooks, the

silent movie star, but I was too shy to tell her, and I didn't
know her well enough to talk about that German film
Pandora's Box in which Louise played the part of a girl who
ended up in the arms of Jack the Ripper. I don't mean at all
that Margaret seemed like a victim, more that she had a
bright and luminous personality, a kind of spiritual quality
which was an odd composition of practicality and flights of
fancy, and in this she was like Rita, and perhaps this heady
mixture was inherent in all Barnsley women and they'd
breathed it in with the coal dust.

I remembered something that Rita had said about the
Labour Party, how it used to be the concern of working men,
how all the family went out canvassing and attended
meetings. Politics then were a part of ordinary folks' lives,
not just the preoccupation of a few militant individuals.

*

My own family were split down the middle, politically, as in
every other way. My mother was a liberal, like her father,
and my Dad was a fervent socialist. My brother and he were
continually at loggerheads over the motorbike which
dripped oil on to the path, his homework, his music practice,
and as a result my brother became a high Tory. My father
was devoted to Joseph Stalin and contemptuous of Winston
Churchill. We ate our tea listening to the six o'clock news
and never a meal went by without a discussion of a political
nature. Other people, my mother for one, might have called
them arguments. Even now, I'm surprised when my own
son, in the middle of what I assume to be a stimulating
exchange of views, declares that he can't stand the shouting.

When I went into the theatre my interest in politics
waned. The actors I worked with were more concerned with
Catholicism than capitalism. Half the cast of the Liverpool
Playhouse were converts to Rome, and I had a crucifix, a
large one made of wood, tucked into my ankle sock. One
night I fainted in the prompt corner during a performance of

Tobias and the Angel. I had a boil on my neck the size of a damson stone and the pain was frightful. I was taken into Maud Carpenter's office and laid on her couch, and Miss Carpenter thought I was carrying a dagger. She said she didn't want me turning eccentric and if I must have a crucifix why didn't I have a normal one and hang it round my neck.

I've never been sure what constitutes eccentricity. When I was a child there was a man called Mr Boriston, who was judged pretty odd even before he lent my father a copy of Swift's *Odes to Stella* – the failing verses, as he foolishly described them in my mother's hearing – but that was because he answered the vicar's rhetorical questions during sermon time and wore his trousers at half mast. On the other hand the vicar was odd on account of the ribbon he tied round his brow when riding his bike. And there was a woman in the village who was rumoured to go to bed in nothing but a pair of gardening gloves, though in her case the oddity lay in her indifference to the cold, seeing that everyone else in those pre-central-heating nights retired in liberty vests and balaclava helmets. The term eccentric only applied to the upper classes; the vicar almost qualified because he'd been to boarding school. Mr Boriston was referred to as queer, which he may have been on top of everything else. The Red Dean, according to my mother, was simply potty.

When I was married and living in Liverpool I became involved again in politics. My husband was a teacher at the art school and he asked Bessie Braddock, who was no oil painting, if she would sit for her portrait. She came to our flat in Catherine Street for several weeks, and though she never bought the completed picture she gave both of us a copy of the *Ragged Trousered Philanthropists*, that book which Mrs Criddle had tried to give me years before. I had had my first baby by the time the Cuban crisis came, and for this reason as much as anything else I was picked to go and protest to the American Consul. I'd rehearsed what I was going to say – a polite but firm demand that he should instruct his President not to do whatever he was thinking of doing – and I walked into his office quite confidently with my son on my hip. I wasn't prepared for the Consul to look like a cross between Gregory Peck and Rasputin and I was struck dumb with admiration. When he said how lovely my baby was, I forgot all about missiles; they were the last thing on my mind.

Three years later I was sent on another delegation. We travelled by coach to London, picking up supporters on the way. I don't know what it was in aid of now, but I do remember the slogan: 'One, two, three, four, Handley Page has locked the door.' I think Handley Page had something to do with aircraft. When we arrived at Victoria I went off to make a phone call home to see if the children had choked in my absence. I had to queue and it must have been at least a quarter of an hour before I returned to the assembly point outside the coach station. And they had gone without me. I had to use my tea money and chase them in a taxi. By this time the procession had swelled; the columns marched in thousands down Victoria Street, banners flying, and all I could see was a forest of bobbing heads, and all I could hear were five thousand voices chanting: 'Two, four, six, eight, we say negotiate.' I never set eyes on our delegation until we met up again at midnight at the coach station. I did get to the Houses of Parliament, and I did join a Scottish contingent, determined to get inside to lobby their MP, but I was chilled by a man in a red scarf who looked up at that Gothic tower and announced that the first thing he would do when he got into power would be to 'smash that bloody wee tick-tock'.

I spent the rest of the evening in a Lyons Corner House with a fellow from Glamorgan who treated me to cheese on toast and said he'd been twelve years of age before he'd owned a pair of shoes, and that was only because his sister had grown out of them.

*

Mark Britton is Geoff's dad, the one who dipped his leg into a pool of melted iron. His father and two older brothers had worked down the pit. After four weeks of the 1926 strike they hadn't a penny left to live on, not one penny. Even before the strike things were hard. It was standard practice to be employed for as little as two days a week. Labour was expendable. If a man was killed down the pit it didn't really matter – there were plenty more – but if a horse was killed, well that was serious, because the coal owners had to pay out brass to buy a new one. During the strike they starved; it was as simple as that. There was no comparison between that strike and this last one. People were inconvenienced this time, of course, but it was more a question of not being able to buy petrol for their cars or keep up the payments on the hi-fi's and the video recorders. It was a matter of doing without chopper-bikes for the kiddies at Christmas and summer holidays in Benidorm. That first time, he and his brothers used to go down to the canal and dive to the bottom to salvage a few lumps of coal that had slipped off the barges, just so that they could have a bit of heat in the house. His dad went back when it was all over, and then in 1936 the seam he was working on gave out; at fifty-six years of age there wasn't a cat in hell's chance of getting another job. It killed him. He died bitter.

Mark went into a foundry. He was really interested in the work, and he supported his family on his wages. His dad was receiving four shillings a week from the authorities, and even then they were coming round and harassing him, snooping about the house, asking him if he owned a piano or anything that wasn't absolutely essential for keeping body and soul together.

He made his first furnace out of an old drum, and as time went by he began to prosper; he got bigger premises and took on staff. At the beginning they cast iron from scrap because they couldn't afford pig-iron. He drew the same wages as the men, and he gave his wife all the money he earned. If he needed something extra for himself he made a few bob as a semi-professional musician. He played the saxophone and the clarinet. A few years back when it looked as though Geoff might lose his sight he bought some farmland. He thought it would be better for Geoff to be out in the open air, even if he was going to tap round it in the dark. He owns ninety acres now and rents it out.

It's a fact, people are bitter round here. They don't forget the past and they teach it to their children. The North has always had a raw deal. 'The richest people live in London. Think on all the money that has gone down there from here. They've got a better climate, better farmland. We've always had to dig up the earth for coal and iron. There isn't a house round here that isn't subsiding. They've got coal in the South but they've never bothered to dig for it.'

It was true about his leg, that he hadn't regretted the accident. Somehow it had concentrated his mind; before that he had relied on his brawn.

*

I suppose progress must always be achieved at the expense of something else. Take communities: they come into existence because people are forced through common circumstances to rely on each other. When the need is removed the community isn't necessary any more.

No matter how poorly most of our children are now educated, or housed, no matter how bleak the unemployment figures, the rise in crime statistics, the decline of our northern cities, it is a fact that we now enjoy a standard of living better than at any time in our history. A minority in this country, North and South, are underprivileged, even though their condition bears no relation to the plight of that desperate majority of the past, but it could be that the consequences of comparative poverty are less debilitating than the effects of general affluence. The greatest changes in the aims of government have usually come about when the majority have been reduced to their knees, and have been achieved not by those kneeling masses but through the efforts of an upright, fanatical few. By and large a nation gets the government it deserves and one which reflects its preoccupations. A government concerned with balancing the books, with oil revenues, with nuclear strategy, is presumably doing what the majority wishes it to do. Politics have always been entangled in morality, for reasons which I don't understand unless it's a throw back to the influence of the church on the state, which could explain why, now religion and the soul and the hereafter are no longer in fashion, heads of government talk as never before in such deeply moralising tones. Mrs Thatcher grieves over the loss of attitudes rooted in and dependent on an oppressed and deprived society; Ronald Reagan extols the buccaneering enterprise of the pioneers who trailed across America. Both leaders are sincere, if sentimental, in their nostalgia. Progress to them, paradoxically, with its heart transplants and Exocets, its sexual revolution and journeys to the stars, its dangerous abandonment of a parochial constitution in favour of a severely organised centralisation, should have led backwards not forwards.

I had a friend in Liverpool called Leah who wanted things to be different and yet stay the same. She had been educated in what she called the University of Life and was sick of what she had learnt. She was the daughter of a watchmaker and she said her mother had carried her as a baby across the wastes of Russia. Her life hadn't been that dreadful; it was more that she was her own worst enemy and a victim of her temperament. She worked for the Labour Party and performed play-readings at Unity Theatre. She fell in love with a married man and after succumbing once to him douched herself with Lysol for twenty years. One winter the pipes of the house she lived in burst and water flooded down the stairs. Her landlord – she called him Eichmann – wanted her evicted and refused to contact the Water Board. He had another house round the corner and he never thought she'd stay. She hung on for three days; it was bitterly cold and the water froze on the stairs, a sheet of ice from hall to landing. Then she gave in and came to stay with me, and I gave up my brass bed and slept on the sofa. She got into bed wearing her black beret and her mackintosh, and then there were scufflings and heavings and I thought she was getting undressed, but all she removed were lengths of bandages, purple with iodine stains, which she flung over the bars of the bed, and all night long she groaned in her sleep and called on God. I asked her what the bandages were for and she said she'd had her uterus removed and did I know that it was the Greek word for hysteria. 'In my case, darling,' she said, 'the knife failed to cut deep enough.'

She talked of making a new start for herself, on the railways at night, travelling backwards and forwards in and out of cities, her face pressed to the window to glimpse those flickering images gone in an instant: a man raising his fist, a woman washing the pots, a figure hunched in a chair. 'Other people are what get me down, darling,' she said. 'I'm so different from them. But if I could just move about in a sitting position and observe them through glass, life would be bearable.'

Had she lived to own a television set she might have changed her mind, for now we all watch without being seen, and what we see, of wars, of famine, triumphs and disasters, merely confirms that other people are ourselves. Yet, faced with this mirror image we continue to categorise each other; rich and poor, good and bad, northerners and southerners, educated and ill-informed.

*

Roy Fellows works in Rita's shop. He was dressing a model in the window of 'Pollyanna' when I met him, draping a checked jacket worth £200 over its waxy shoulders, fixing its wig in place. Outside, the women of Barnsley were hurrying along the pavement clutching their purses and wheeling their babies in push-chairs.

What do you think in the head, I wonder, when you keep being told that the North is in decline and that there'll be nothing for your children to do when they're grown? Do you look into those shop windows and dream, or do you see in those perfectly featured mannequins a reflection of those remote and alien beings who rule from the South, who posture behind the glass of the television screen talking of economic factors and budgets and global considerations?

Roy left Barnsley at eighteen to go to Reading University to read history of art. He switched to sociology in mid-course and later went to Cambridge to study criminology. He would have stayed in the South if it had not been for a car crash which left his girl-friend Lynn paralysed and brain-damaged. He returned to Barnsley because he needed the support of his family to help look after her. With the insurance money they've just bought a wing or two of Birthwaite Hall, a manor house on a rise of ground beyond the village in which he was born.

He was down there earlier this morning, planning what to do with the neglected grounds. It's obvious that he'll tackle the problem with the same thoroughness he would have brought to a career in politics or the law. In one section he wants a stretch of garden laid out in the English cottage tradition – herbs and wild flowers and nothing too orderly. The lower terraces are a little short on colour but they don't require anything too garish. There's a great big beech in the centre of the lawn which casts a shadow on the grass, and they could put more bulbs in there. Something will have to be done eventually about the choked waterfall beyond the expanse of daffodils and bluebells, and the two lily ponds will need draining and starting up again from scratch. Perhaps the basic theme of the lower garden ought to be centred round shrubs. The wild onion plants look nice and should be saved but some of the rhododendrons could be cut out. As for the wilderness of the orchard, he'll leave it for now and get a goat in later. They need more roses planted on the top terrace, and of course the path will have to be levelled off because of Lynn and her wheel-chair.

It had been difficult, he said, coming back home. People had thought him potty for leaving in the first place, and then when he returned he was regarded as a failed southener. When he went out to a pub or met with friends and they got talking, even about something as unimportant as television, and he tried to introduce a new way of looking at things – nothing revolutionary, simply less predictable – he could tell they thought he was cracked. They pitied him for coming back, as if it was only those who had been beaten who limped home with their tails between their legs. In a sense he was lost in the middle of two cultures. Down South he had been taken for a token northerner, the 'eeh bah gum' sort of music-hall turn, and up here, when he moves his hands to express himself or shows too deep an interest in fashion he's taken for a poof.

'There's no cultural entertainment in Barnsley,' he said, 'because of its close position to Manchester, and Sheffield has the Crucible Theatre and Leeds has opera. Barnsley is a kind of stepping-off stone to other places. There was an American tourist a while back who asked an old chap if there was a museum round here that he could visit. "Yes," said the old man, quick as a flash, "sixteen pits and they're all closed." That's what's wrong with Barnsley now, and it's duplicated all over England, not just in the North. It's lack of continuity. Take my own village – there used to be a pit at either end, and Long Row had a hundred and fifty houses and every man living in them worked at the mines. Then the pits closed and now it's just fields with the grass growing over the lumps. People left the area, or at least most of them did, and now nobody hardly knows anyone. Before, you could walk down the street and call everybody by name. And it's getting rough down there, like all the places in England – like York on a Saturday night, and Reading and Slough and Doncaster – and it's because there's no self-policing any more, no knowledge or shared interest in each other, because the population keeps being split up and shifted on to council estates. Up to twenty years ago society was based on communities, and now they've broken up people haven't yet learnt how to cope. Life is too small suddenly, too lonely.'

His father, Mr Fellows, was an ice-cream man who later became a coal merchant. Roy's brother David has taken over the business.

'Our David could have gone to university if he'd wanted to – he was clever enough – but he wouldn't even go to grammar school. He passed the exam but he refused to wear a snobby uniform. He's exceptionally good at maths, and it's not wasted because he has a scientific approach to betting on the horses.'

*

I was never any good at maths because I never grasped its principles. I hadn't been taught properly. There were three streams in my class and I was always in the bottom one. One time, during an exam, I was given in error a question paper which was meant for the top stream, and I kept it and quite happily attempted it. The teacher thought that I had been insolent in not pointing out the mix-up, that I was playing silly beggars, but I hadn't noticed. It was an algebra paper, and we hadn't got that far in the lower stream, but all maths was Greek to me and I just thought the questions were more incomprehensible than usual, though if anything it seemed a bit easier dealing with letters rather than numbers, and I enjoyed guessing at what the answers might be. It was the maths teacher who wouldn't stand up for me when a meeting was called to decide whether I should be expelled or not. It was her fault just as much as Miss Smith's that I was.

It was my fourteenth birthday and as a treat my mother was going to take me out for a knife-and-fork tea and then to the Playhouse to see a performance of *Dr Faustus*. I went straight from school, going up on the train from Crosby to Exchange Station to meet her under the clock in the booking hall. The moment I set eyes on her, saw her face beneath her hat brimmed with roses, I knew something was wrong. It seemed that all my life I had been waiting to be caught out at something, and now I had been, though what it was I couldn't tell. She was very quiet and severe, and she kept looking at me sideways in a funny calculating way as if she'd never seen me before, and little beads of terror rolled through my head.

I hardly tasted my tea. We had ham and chips and bread and butter and it might all have been made of cardboard. She kept clearing her throat as if to make some pronouncement but all she said were things like, 'Sit up straight' and 'Stop kicking the table.'

I didn't really like going to the theatre. You had to keep still and I was sure the actors could see me in the darkness, and it was tiring having to look interested and animated. Even then, I was always bothered about people making fools of themselves and having to be sorry for them, and my mouth ached with smiling my appreciation. The only time I had ever gone to the theatre and not cared about keeping up appearances was at a showing of the *Student Prince* at the Royal Court Theatre; they were all so frenzied and pleased with themselves, banging their tankards on the tables in golden Heidelberg and slapping each other on the back that my participation wasn't necessary.

In the middle of the second act, after Faustus had sold his soul to the Devil, there was a scene depicting the seven deadly sins. I understood Greed and Sloth, but then a woman came on in a tattered evening frock and writhed all over the dusty stage. 'What's Lechery?' I asked my mother in a whisper. I was really interested. My mother said, 'I should have thought you'd have known the answer to that, Beryl.' She never called me by my name, certainly not on my birthday. I was always her little chickie or her sausage, and I was terrified.

She didn't say anything coming out of the theatre nor walking up Stanley Street to the station, and the Devil went with us every step of the way. We sat in silence as the train rocked through the darkness, past Seaforth and Bootle and Blundellsands. I pressed my nose to the window and pretended to be looking out at the black sea, but I was watching her profile reflected in the glass, her eyes staring at me, her mouth turned down. Then she told me, half way between Hallroad and Hightown.

After breakfast she had put my gymslip into the wash and found a piece of paper in that fatal pocket. I had no defence. I had written down some verses of a naughty rhyme told to my by Rita Moody. I was good at art and I had illustrated them. My mother had rung up the school immediately and told the headmistress, who had asked her to come and see her that same afternoon. It was that important. I could infect the whole school, a rotten apple in the barrel.

When the train reached Formby my dog Pedro was waiting for me under the lamp on the corner by the council offices. He bounded towards me, and then, as if sensing my mother's disapproval, he slunk down and let me pass, not wanting to be contaminated.

We entered the house by the front door, which was peculiar; usually we went up the side path to the scullery to save the carpet in the hall. I went straight upstairs and hung about on the landing. It was freezing and I tried opening the airing-cupboard in the bathroom to get warm and some of the dahlia tubers fell out and rolled across the floor. My brother called out, 'Is that you, Beryl?' and I said, 'Yes, what do you want?' and he said, 'Nothing, nothing from you. You're beyond the pale.'

My parents weren't speaking downstairs and I didn't know if I could go to bed. I hadn't a room of my own and I wasn't sure if I'd be allowed in my mother's bed seeing I was so degenerate.

The next day I was in the gardens of the school with my best friend, rummaging in the flower beds for treasure, when Miss Johnson the biology teacher came up and said the headmistress wanted to talk to me. I'd only ever seen her before on the platform in prayers or in the corridor, and she seemed smaller face to face and much redder in complexion. She said that there were some things in life that were very beautiful and sacred and mustn't be trampled on. I thought she meant the flower beds and I said I hadn't stood on them, and she told me that I must make a great effort to cleanse my heart. I just sat there, looking at the papers on her desk; outside, I could hear my friends shrieking beneath the windows, pulling leaves from their bottoms as they played at having babies. When she had finished her chat the headmistress gave me a book about bees.

*

Later that afternoon I went to visit Roy's Mum and Dad in their bungalow in Carlton Village. Roy was still talking.

'I don't know whether it was the university that changed me,' he said, 'or going to a university in the South. All I know is, I went there because I felt life must have more to offer.'

'But you're not doing much now,' said his mother. 'At least, you're not doing what you were trained for, what you went to college for.'

'I've told you,' Roy said. 'You don't go to university for a set thing. You go to broaden your outlook. It's not like an apprenticeship when you come out having only learnt what is relevant to your trade. I know you think of the fashion industry as airy-fairy, but don't forget it's one of the major employers of this country. I wouldn't mind getting into the managerial side. My skills are basically organisational.'

'When he came back from being down South,' said Joan Fellows, 'he was quite different. He was very fussy when he was little about his clothes and yet he hadn't been at the university five minutes before he threw all that out of the window and wore nothing but second-hand articles.'

'I wasn't the only one,' protested Roy.

'Look at his spectacles,' his mother urged.

'What's wrong with them?' asked Roy.

'They've got coloured rims,' she said. 'You'd think he'd been brought up in France, wouldn't you, the way he keeps waving his hands. You should have seen the state of him when he came back for the holidays.'

'Everybody had long hair then,' said Roy.

'He brought a friend home with him that first time, and he had hair right down his back. His name was Julian, but we didn't know that until he'd left. We took him for a lass and we called him Gillian.'

'It's true,' Roy said.

'You went down to do history of art and then you switched,' accused his mother.

'It's allowed,' said Roy. 'Lots of people switch. That's what the system's for.'

'Even when he was little he could never stick at one thing for very long. He was always changing his mind. I'll grant you he was artistic, right from the start. Drawing things and making clothes for his dolls.'

'Dolls?' said Roy.

'Those action men,' she said. 'He was always asking for bits of material to make new outfits for them.'

Mr Fellows didn't get much of a chance to express his views. He sat well back on the sofa and looked from his wife to his son and kept his thoughts to himself. Both Roy and his mother were in agreement that Barnsley had changed, and for the worse. Mrs Fellows thought it had a lot to do with the local councillors all being yes-men and not being paid salaries. 'They should throw the whole lot out and start again,' she said. They shouldn't be party members. They shouldn't be influenced by the trade unions.'

'But the Conservative Party is influenced by the managerial bosses,' said Roy. 'You don't complain about that.'

'It's easy for you to talk,' his Mum argued. 'You haven't been here. You didn't have to deal with it.'

'You can't bring up lack of experience as an argument,' countered Roy.

'Yes, I can.'

'No, you can't. There's no other country in Europe in which being a communist is equated with being a mass-murderer. The Labour councillors lack vision because they're uneducated, as are most of the English working-class. If you're a socialist in the old meaning of the term you're treated as if you've got herpes or Aids. The Labour party manifesto of 1945 was far more radical than the one put out by Michael Foot, and where did it get him? The working-class are politically ignorant because they get their opinions from the gutter press. It was the same press that broke the strike, giving the wrong statistics and implying that morale was low. It wasn't like that at all, but reading what those papers printed you'd have thought the miners were all on their knees. The only paper that told the truth was the Manchester Guardian, and for a short while a minority of the miners were politically informed and read a decent newspaper because it was the only one they recognised as reporting the facts as they were. Arthur Scargill led a march through Barnsley. He should have led it through London. We knew what the strike was all about. It's all very well for people down South to say that the mines should be closed because they're unprofitable, but do they

realise that the consequences of that is that they'll be paying
the miners not to work for the next twenty years? If that
was explained a bit more clearly, I think it would put a
different complexion on the matter. Where's the oil revenue
gone? It was supposed to be the saving of us. I'll tell you
where it's gone – it's been squandered on paying
unemployment benefit to three and a half million on the
dole. Len Murray took a knighthood for it. Look at the
Falklands – nobody knew where they were until she sent the
gun-boats out '

'Yes, they did,' cried his Mum. 'Our Malcolm's been
there.'

It was night-time now and almost dark. Soon the blazing
star above King Arthur's pit would hang in the sky like a
brooch. The ravaged land was turning black. In twenty years
the scars will have healed, on the landscape at least. Unlike
man, the earth grows young with every spring. The rutted
tracks on this battlefield of industrial England will be lost in
grass-soaked meadows, and only the miners will remember
that here they stood their shifting ground, dazzled by
dreams of Camelot. Dependent on where you live, or how
you vote, the expansion of the South and the contraction of
the North is seen either as an unnatural result of deliberate
policies, or as the accidental effect of natural forces.

If you come from the North as I do, and you left it, as I
did, you have ambivalent feelings towards the old working
communities. It's an uneasy mixture of pride and irritation,
sentimentality and mistrust, for you broke away from a
narrowness of outlook and a lack of expectation which
well-nigh crushed you. And yet – the heart lies back there in
the past, and everyone longs to return and find things just as
they were, the arguments in full spate and the home-fires
still burning.

4

The Powells of Bentley

Bentley is near Farnham, on the ancient road from Southampton to London. Travelling there by train from Waterloo one passes Wimbledon and Byfleet, Woking and Aldershot, through pleasant fields and the remains of forests. Bentley has some cottages, a few splendid old houses, a medieval church, a pond with ducks and a Memorial hall, but to the casual visitor these are all so scattered that it doesn't seem like a village, and in any case the A31 runs straight through it. On the main road, next to the bus stop, is something called the Bentley Sign, housed in a sort of thatched grotto with a dwarf wearing tennis shoes perched on top, brandishing a broken bow and arrow. Baden Powell – no relation to the Powells – was responsible for this – the Bentley Sign, that is, not the broken bow. The Chief Scout came to the village in 1919 and lived for twenty years in a house called Pax Hill. He endowed the Memorial hall, founded the Fly-Fishing Association and designed the Bentley grotto for the *Daily Mail* Village Signs Competition of 1924.

Christine Powell was born in London at the beginning of the First World War. Her family moved to Surrey when she was six years old. 'So I've always been a country person,' she said. Her father had been a wine merchant and had travelled a lot.

'Those were the early days of the aeroplane,' she explained, 'and my father loved flying. My mother was terrified of it, and he used to hide from her the fact that he'd just flown to France or to Germany, but she could always tell because he came back deaf. Planes made such a noise in those days.'

Christine and I were walking under an autumn sky round

and round a perfect English garden, discussing families and roses.

'That's an Etoile d'Hollande climber,' she said, pointing at a magnificent rambler which clung to the back of the red brick house beyond the yew hedge. 'And that's a Caroline Testout. They both have second flowerings. You need a rose that flowers twice in a season.'

There was something I was trying to remember, some submerged memory of the past in which I had walked through a similar garden, heavy with the scent of roses, and come to a patch of lawn gone bald and heard a voice complaining about rabbits.

'I've been in a garden like this before,' I told Christine. 'Though I can't remember where.' I began to wonder if it wasn't a photograph that I was seeing in my mind – the grounds of the Sitwells' house, Renishaw, with the gardener posed beside the hundred-headed lily.

'I loathed botany at school,' Christine said. 'It was my worst subject. All those wretched stamens. Now, I love planting and potting and contrasting one colour with another. It's very satisfying, don't you think?'

'Did you know you'd have this sort of life?' I asked. 'You know, gardens and things?'

'I've been very lucky,' she said. 'I'm conscious of it. Some people have very bad luck.' She'd had a happy childhood and been devoted to both parents, though possibly her father had been the greatest influence. Not having any sons, he'd taken her to rugger matches. He was a great sportsman – golf and tennis and rugger, and he'd played cricket with W.G. Grace. There was a photograph, somewhere in the house, of the two of them together. And she'd enjoyed school, unlike some who didn't seem able to remember those days without shuddering, but she supposed that was because she had been what one would call a hockey-playing miss. Her father was such a wise man, a good man. Not terrifically intellectual or anything like that, but full of sound judgment and sense. People went to him for advice, and he was fun as well. She'd admired him. Both her parents had been keen on education. She would have liked to have been a doctor but had never got round to it, though she had qualified as a dietician at King's College. 'I've been very lucky,' she repeated. 'My childhood, the fact that I had a husband after the war. Most of the men in Patrick's squadron were killed.' The war had changed her, but then, that sort of catastrophe changed everybody. 'One's thinking was influenced ... you met people you wouldn't have done otherwise ... you began to question what it was all about ... that sort of thing.' Then she showed me another species of rose, a Charles Austin, one that she thought was possibly her favourite.

It comes to us all, with age, this preoccupation with the soil, with seed packets and cuttings. When I was working in a bottle factory I was foolish enough to confide in the Italian cellar manager that I was interested in gardening. 'Ah,' he enthused. 'Such joy in the hand-made vegetable. What is to compare with a tomato he himself alone has uplifted?'

What indeed, I had agreed, though in this case *she* herself had never managed to raise anything more joyous than a few raddled sweet peas and half a dozen rampant marigolds. The manager was determined to be helpful – it had something to do with peasant thrift and his Mamma hanging garlic sausages from a hook in the kitchen ceiling back home in Palermo – and in no time at all he had brought me some lettuce seedlings to plant in my backyard. He'd hardly gone out of the front gate before the sparrows swooped like hawks and ate the lot. When told of this tragedy he tut-tutted and returned with a second crop which suffered the same fate as the first. I was embarrassed because I knew he'd pop in again to see how they were doing. I ran round to Marks and Spencer and spent the family allowance on real lettuces. There wasn't time to dig them in deeply and I was afraid he might fondle them and find they were rootless.

Every time he bent too close to the earth I shrieked and said a wasp was after me. He said I had green limbs.

'Gardening allows one plenty of time to think,' observed Christine. 'It leaves the mind free.'

We had been on our way to the potting shed for the best part of half an hour, but there were so many plants to see, so many blooms to admire that we still hadn't got there. Regularly we waved at Patrick who was sitting in his wellies under an arbour of flowering pear.

'How did you two meet?' I asked Christine, when we had drawn level with him for perhaps the third time.

'At a dance,' she said, 'before the war,' and she picked me a rose called Ophelia to wear in my buttonhole. I hoped it wasn't an omen; earlier I had walked round the village pond which was bright green though thick with ducks.

'And did you start going out together right away?' I persisted.

'No,' she said. 'Quite soon after we met I went to Egypt with my father, and then on to Kenya. I was away for three months. We got married just before the war really got started. We were lucky in that too. Most people had to put up with a rather makeshift affair, but we had a lovely wedding. Actually, we had met once before, at a tennis party at the house of friends, but Patrick doesn't remember.'

'What's that?' called Patrick, hearing his name.

'I was talking of the time we first met, darling. The time you don't remember.'

'Oh, that time,' he said. 'I remember the dance all right.'

'Perhaps you should speak to Patrick,' Christine said, and she escaped to the potting shed.

'She gets frightfully bored with me telling that story,' confided Patrick.

'I won't be,' I said.

'Well, it was at dinner at a friend's house before going on to the Old Sherborne Girls' dance in aid of the Mission – Christine had been at Sherborne – and I was standing at the fireplace talking to my hostess when Christine came in with her escort. I turned to my hostess and I said, who's that girl? I shall marry her. Quite extraordinary. I often feel that my life has gone according to some plan – the fact that I survived the war when all the odds were against it. Anyway, I managed to get the last dance with her, though she had to leave early because her father was dining nearby and came to motor her home. I asked her out once after that, and then she went off up the Nile. I sent flowers to the ship. I'm quite sure Christine thought I was just another flighty young man, but I'd never done that sort of thing in my life before – sending flowers and all that – and I haven't done it very often since. I wasn't any good at that sort of thing. A result of the public schools, I suppose. I didn't find it easy to show my feelings.'

I was thinking of my father, and how his trouble had been that he had never been able to hide his. All his emotions were just under his skin. He took umbrage on the slightest excuse, was moved to tears at the sound of a sentimental song. He had no reticence. My mother said it was on account of his puritanical upbringing. He'd never been encouraged to study himself in the mirror; he was too fond of curling his lip and flaring his nostrils. He had no conception of the exaggeration of his gestures, of the theatricality of his facial expressions.

'I remember talking to a headmaster of a school in Australia,' Patrick was saying. 'He said it was his opinion that one feature of a boy from the boarding-school system was his inability to express himself, to let himself go. I'd never given much thought to it before.' He himself had loved school. He had been a natural. Some people, of course, had hated it. It had suited him because he was lonely at home – his sister was ten years older than he and his brother had died. He didn't think his mother had liked sending him away but she had accepted it because it was the form to do so. Besides, boarding school had stopped him from being spoilt. At school everyone was treated the same, whether they came from a castle or a suburban villa. After coming down from Cambridge he had joined his father's stock-broking firm. He hadn't encouraged either of his own sons to go into the business because he didn't believe the prospects would be the same in a socialist era. 'I enjoyed my days on the floor,' he said. 'It was tremendous fun. I started out collecting cheques and doing clerical work. Then I became a blue button and ran messages. My cousin John and I took over the firm eventually, and I retired ten years ago. We were very lucky. We had planned a merger, and just at the right time we were approached with the right offer and taken over by Laing & Cruickshank. You see what I mean by my life working to some plan?'

I confessed that I didn't understand the machinations of the Stock Exchange and he said it had all changed, become too big, though, of course, that sort of thing was necessary now that everything was international. It amazed him really, all this talk of jobbers and brokers and dual capacity being the great thing to aim for, and yet Lloyds was doing the exact opposite. It was extraordinary.

I wanted to know if his sons, Bruce and Martin, had enjoyed school in the way he had done. He thought they probably had. They had both been naturals too, and very good at games. Of course they got that from Christine's side of the family. Her father and uncle, J.H. and A.F. Todd, had been excellent sportsmen, one a Scottish rugger international and the other regularly playing cricket with W.G. Grace. They had both played with W.G. as a matter of fact, and there was a photograph hanging up somewhere taken of the three of them. One of the Todd brothers had been a friend of Apsley Cherry Gerrard, that gentle man who had gone with Scott to the Pole, and who, after surviving temperatures of minus 65 degrees on nothing more than a few digestive biscuits, had brought home an egg of the emperor penguin only to be told by an official at the door of the British Museum that they weren't running a grocer's shop. The poor fellow died mad, but it was men of that calibre, steel all through, that the public schools produced. Little Louis, Bruce's son, had it in him too, the sporting instinct, that is; you can tell by the way he moves. He's only two, but he runs beautifully. Bruce had gone away to school when he was eight, and Martin when he was eight. Christine had gone to collect one or other of them at the end of his first term and when he saw her he called her Ma'am, because that's what Matron was called. Christine had been horrified. Both Christine and Lizzie, Bruce's wife, were anti-boarding school for very young children. He had no doubt that it might not suit some, but for the majority of boys it could only be of value to receive a degree of male discipline, be away from Mother's apron strings. He didn't believe either of his daughters-in-law, Lizzie or Rosie, agreed with him, but then they probably hadn't enjoyed school.

*

That horrible little man, Flogging Keate, a former headmaster of Eton, was a male disciplinarian par excellence; he birched anything that moved. One would have imagined that such inhuman treatment would have rendered his pupils incapable of learning, or rather that knowledge would have been imprinted on something lower than the brain, but the reverse seems to have been the case. There is a story that when Pitt in the House of Commons was interrupted in the middle of a quotation from the *Aeneid*, the whole House, Whigs and Tories alike, rose as one man to supply the end. My poor schoolmaster, Mr Watson, left some lines of Latin on his desk following the battering of his wife, and the letter page of *The Times* was occupied for weeks with correspondence from 'old boys' tormenting themselves over the correct translation of his hastily scribbled note, M.H.C. maintaining that the phrase *olim amanti* involved a contradiction in terms and C.H. of Camden Town wondering, in the bloody circumstances, whether Watson's handwriting hadn't been at fault. Had he perhaps meant to write not *amare* (to love) but *amari* (to be loved), not *amanti* (lover) but *amenti* (madman), and was it not merely an epigram to the tale *Hercules*, a work which he had been labouring on at the time of his wife's murder? It is to be hoped that C.H. was right. The mind boggles at the thought of a man explaining his reasons for such an act in an obscure language. It is reported that the Cabinet of the time was divided on the issue of Watson's Latin, and it is not impossible that the same thing could happen today, for men from the same educational establishments still hold political power. The Lord Chancellor is an old Etonian, as are Lord Carrington, Francis Pym and Ian Gilmore. Willie Whitelaw and Geoffrey Howe went to Winchester, James Prior to Charterhouse, Keith Joseph to Harrow. Listen to any man in the bath who is warbling the Eton boating song and he'll turn out to be a director of the clearing banks, the discount houses or the merchant banks. It may be bad luck on the rest of the male population who never went to such schools, but it can't be a bad thing to be ruled by men who know the difference between a lover and a lunatic.

I was sent away to boarding school at fourteen, after Miss Smith and her gymslip pocket had precipitated my expulsion from Merchant Taylors. My mother wanted me to go to RADA, but it would have meant that I would have had to live in digs. Instead, she found the Cone-Ripman Ballet School in Tring. My father saw me off at Lime Street, making sure that I was in a carriage with two old ladies, but even as the guard blew his whistle four sailors with kitbags burst into the compartment. My father trotted alongside the moving train, gesticulating, his melancholy eyes glittering under the brim of his Homburg hat.

I went by coach from Euston to Tring. It was winter and dark by the time I reached the school. My mother had had my hair permanently waved the week before and it was the same texture as my school coat. The bus turned off the road into a drive and there were the shapes of trees and a notice board showing faintly. We ate eggs on toast in a basement which might have been a dungeon, and there were long loaves of bread with wet insides, and most of the girls seemed elderly and lit cigarettes after the meal. One girl had bunches of yellow curls hanging like grapes over her ears. She wore a clever, amused expression, and after yawning she said, 'My God, I'm tired.' Then we walked in the darkness outside, under some trees and through a door that had horseshoes nailed up all over it, and up some stone steps to a room with three beds. The girl with the clever face said I had better make up my bed, and another girl came in and began to eat an onion. I turned my back and fiddled with my bedding and looked at the name tapes my mother had sewn on to the blankets, and tears came into my eyes because I didn't know how to make a bed. In the end I had to turn round and the onion-eater said, 'Aren't you the girl that hasn't had any schooling?' in a funny sprawled voice – a South African take-me-back-to-the-old-Transvaal sort of voice. I said 'Yes.' She must have been mixing me up with someone else, because I'd hardly had a beastly day off school for years; but it was easier than saying that I hadn't got a bed of my own at home and that I slept with my mother, and that she always made the bed anyway, and that my brother slept with my father and the dog. This girl, who turned out to be quite nice, and who used to break into the Prince Igor dances at the drop of a hat, helped me to make the bed. The other one lay down and continued to yawn.

After three days, in which I didn't do any schooling and hardly anything else but hide in the Elizabethan gardens, the mistake was discovered and I was removed from the stables and placed in the main school. I had been mixed up with a girl who had lived in Kenya and run wild in the jungle.

There's very little about my schooldays that I remember now, except the snow coming down one winter Sunday when we went to church. In the square the Salvation Army was playing 'The Sea of Love is Rolling In'. It was a bit like a Christmas card and I think I felt like crying. I don't mean I was homesick or anything. It was just that sentimental moments like that, the snow and the hymns, made me feel pleasantly sad. Anyway, I remember that particular morning because later, during the service, I didn't kneel down quickly enough and Matron thwacked me on the shoulder with her umbrella and I almost swung round and bashed her. Not that I minded about the umbrella, but I'd been day-dreaming about the vicar, alternating between thinking he was Rochester and I was Jane Eyre (What, leave Thornfield and all that I hold most dear?) and the idea of him being Charles Boyer in that film about the Titanic. We were sinking together with the violins playing – I had refused to get into the boats – and Matron spoilt it all with her brolly tapping.

I was too old, I think, too set in my provincial ways to get much out of boarding school. I might have come from another planet, let alone another part of the country. I had the impression I spoke another language, which indeed I did, and that I was larger than anyone else, stuck out more, didn't fit in. They said my nails were dirty, my voice was rough; sometimes they even laughed at my face, and in those moments I knew that I looked like my father and that I was twisting my mouth and contorting my brow and generally playing the clown. Like him, I had no control. And I was still ready to use my fists, which I can see now was a bit extreme, but had passed for normal behaviour in the playground at Blundellsands or on the station platform at Formby. I didn't use bad language, and when I consider the swearing which had gone on at home this was jolly balanced of me, but I did flare up when faced with authority and petty rules about not using other people's tooth-brushes. I couldn't find my level, and this was odd because circumstances had made me very adaptable. Criticisms in the past had been for different reasons; I understood I was verbally awkward. Following a scripture lesson at Merchant Taylors on the Beatitudes we had been asked if we had any questions, and I had said, 'What's VD?' That was being awkward. But in Tring such a question was reasonable and had it been asked it would have been answered. So all I had to fall back on was either emotion or aggression and neither seemed to rate very high in Tring.

In the beginning, mostly it seems to me because of my fingernails, I was detested by both staff and pupils, which made me stubborn, and halfway through I became excessively popular, which made me a show-off. I couldn't get over the size of the school house which had been built by Charles II for Nell Gwyn, whose library was lined with oak from Nelson's battleship, any more than I could get over being sent off to bed at half past eight, when at home I had roamed the shore until midnight in double summer time. My aptitude for ballet remained stationary; I thought it silly – if God had meant us to pirouette on our big toes etc. – though my tap-dancing, learnt first from the silver screen and later from Miss Thelma Broadbent in Southport, improved. As for education, gaps remained as wide as ever. I only wanted to know bibs and bobs of things, a verse here, a half line there – 'Now more than ever seems it rich to die, to cease upon the midnight with no pain;' or 'Ah, love, let us be true to one another, for the world which seems to lie before us like a land of dreams etc.' or again, 'Hector's slaves masturbated, as through half-shut doors they watched Andromache astraddle, astride her hubby horse,' – though I was careful not to copy this latter piece into my notebook. What I did learn, in that brief year, was to be less loud, less belligerent. 'Modulate your voice,' my teachers constantly told me. 'The world's not deaf.' Not true, but still, I had spent most of my life trying to make myself heard above voices raised in anger, and shouting was the only way I knew of expressing myself. For the rest, that Tom Brown land of bun-feasts and playing fields eluded me. We weren't allowed to play games in case we hurt our dancing legs.

*

It was quite true, Lizzie Powell said, she hadn't enjoyed being sent away to school. For one, she had adored her mother, and for another the convent she went to in Umtali hadn't taught her a thing. The nuns were all very warm and loving but she was uneducated when she left. She had lived on a farm in Suffolk until she was eight, and then her family moved to Rhodesia, to another farm. Her parents were Catholics and she had eleven brothers and sisters.

I was talking to Lizzie in her house four miles from Bentley. It was a large house, well furnished and well kept, with a man up a ladder painting the windowsills, and a big and pleasant garden. She and Bruce Powell have three daughters and a son, the athletic Louis.

'I gave up being a Catholic,' Lizzie said, 'after having three babies in two-and-a-half years. It was my body and I just thought, why should I go on having babies? I knew it was expected of me, by the Church, I mean, but I couldn't go along with it.' And then, she didn't want to be like her mother. Her mother had been a wonderful person, full of life and charm, and yet she had married at twenty-one and in a sense she had never grown up, had just gone on having babies and being involved in children until she died. 'It's not that I think she wasted her life, it's just that she never experienced anything else other than having children, and I think that's a shame.' When they were small they were all taught at home, mostly because the nearest Catholic school was too far away. When her mother died of cancer their next-door neighbour took over the teaching of the younger children, but by then Lizzie was at the convent. 'I think sending children away to boarding school makes them go on worshipping their parents long after it's natural to do so. Anyway, I don't think boarding school does anything for girls. By and large all the women I know are uneducated. I

116

won't send mine away, not unless they actually insist.'

'And what about Louis?' I asked.

Lizzie said that might well turn out to be a different matter. She had friends who had sons and by the time they were twelve or thirteen their mothers were always having rows with them. And Bruce had loved school. 'I don't want to start having arguments with Louis,' Lizzie said. 'Bruce is away twelve hours a day and there are three girls in the family and I think Louis will need boys around him.' In an ideal world it would be nice if Bruce could work part-time and share in bringing up the children. She had asked him to often enough but he said it wouldn't fulfil him, and really it was unfair of her to expect such a thing when she hadn't made it clear what she wanted in the first place, before they were married. But then, at that stage she hadn't known what she wanted.

Bruce is an accountant with the publishing firm of Octopus. He travels up to London by train every day and doesn't get home much before eight o'clock in the evening. One night a week he stays up in town at the flat of a friend. He'd like Louis to go to Eton as he did because it's the best education there is and he wants his son to have the same advantages. 'Bruce left school thinking everyone was like himself,' Lizzie said. 'Before going up to Cambridge he took a year off and went to Australia. It was a terrible shock for him. He got a job as a deck apprentice on a cargo ship; one of his jobs was to look after ten dogs. He spent most of his time running after them with a shovel. He made the mistake of talking about his background and the crew gave him a bad time. When he came back he said he understood why people were put off by a so-called southern accent – it sounds so confident and toffee-nosed somehow.'

She herself didn't feel qualified to talk about a North/South divide. All she knew was that she and Bruce were incredibly privileged, and what she wanted for herself, what Bruce wanted, was to bring up their children to be

loving and caring people who'd understand the responsibilities that being advantaged entailed. It sounded
pompous but it was true. Beyond that she'd like to achieve
something, she wasn't sure what. Recently she had sat
A-level English and passed with an 'A'. It was the most
exciting thing that had ever happened to her, except for
having children. It was the first thing she had ever done off
her own bat. She wanted to be educated, to be able to speak
knowledgeably on a given subject. She feels that most of her
opinions don't count because she hasn't been to university.
Time and time again she goes to dinner parties and the
person next to her asks what she does, and she says, Oh, I've
got four children, and they say Oh, really, and then turn
away to talk to the person on the other side about something
really important, like money or politics. She feels she has no
merit because housewives don't get paid, and besides, she
hasn't got any qualifications, no bits of paper apart from her
A-level.

I asked her if she missed being a Catholic, and she said of
course she did. She missed that feeling of going to church
and knowing that God was there. 'And there's guilt,
obviously. Catholics always feel guilty, about everything,
and particularly if they're women – not in the Edmund
Gosse sense that God will put you in hell because you've
abandoned Him, but in the sense that you're not good
enough for Him.' She supposed that basically she was an
unhappy person who was happy.

*

I know what Lizzie meant about guilt although mine, in spite
of my conversion to Rome, is of the protestant sort and has
much to do with not feeling good enough for my parents, let
alone God. My conversion began when I was thirteen, after
seeing two paintings by Filippo Lippi in the Southport Art

Gallery. This led directly to the crucifix down my ankle sock. Gibbon rated sixteen a dangerous age and blamed his seduction by Rome on a blind and youthful taste for exotic literature, but though I later read *The Heart of the Matter* and *The End of the Affair*, neither book had the same shattering effect on me as had Lippi and his hang-dog saints with those fanatical eyes whose gaze reminded me of my father.

I had to wait until I was nineteen to change my faith. In England, then, one's religion couldn't be altered under the age of twenty-one without parental consent; the same law didn't apply in Scotland. So it was while I was with the Dundee repertory company that I began to take instruction, hoping in the beginning to be involved in desperate theological discussions, not to say arguments, concerning doubts and dogma. My instructor was a very old nun who had been 'inside' since she was fourteen, and at eighty was long past the doubting stage, or indeed long past anything remotely approaching a discussion, for she was also very deaf. All she could do was murmur at me, her hand making little jumps in the air as though urging me to take that leap into an act of faith. And so I did, six weeks later, mainly because it would have been rude, a waste of the nun's time, not to have done so.

My embracing of the church was to have given me an inner peace, a shield against temptation, but conditions were unfavourable to say the least, as only the week before the producer of the theatre company had been asked to leave, and out of loyalty to him three members of the cast, myself included, had left too. Our leaving hadn't taken us very far, for pending an Equity enquiry our wages had been withheld and we didn't have the train fares home. We were holed up in a bungalow on the mud flats beneath the girders of the Tay Bridge with nothing to eat but sardines and cocoa. Within twenty-four hours of being received into the church I was in a state of mortal sin again, though my abrupt fall from grace was a matter of expediency rather than frailty.

The producer's dismissal had been brought about by a number of factors. There were the disastrous box-office takings during the run of *The Beaver Coat* by Gerhart Hauptmann, a play mainly concerned with an animal called a roebuck. The text had been translated by a Liverpudlian and the actors were required to speak with broad Lancashire accents. My name was Adelheidt and my opening speech began, 'Ma, shall I skin the roebuck?' The next play was a translation from the French and equally incomprehensible to a Scottish audience in that the leading lady couldn't remember her lines. Her inability to do so was caused partly through having fallen in love with the producer, which wrecked her concentration, and partly through exhaustion. On a Sunday we used to walk through the surrounding countryside with suitcases full of books – you couldn't get a drink unless you were a bona fide traveller – and the producer made her carry the luggage. She was always sighing or crying because he preferred young men. One way and another she was a bit of a dumbo – she had already had two husbands, and neither of them had liked girls either. Once, on the bridge of Kirriemuir, she said she was going to throw herself into the water – she was playing the Infanta of Navarre that week – but there was only a trickle of a stream below and she was wearing new shoes. The producer was momentarily upset; he was a kindly man, drenched in Cologne, and he draped his duffel coat about her heaving shoulders and was nice to her for a whole afternoon, dabbing at her tear-stained cheeks with his cashmere scarf and assuring her he wasn't worthy of the gesture.

Then there was the stage director who went temporarily insane and lay down across the tramlines in front of the theatre and had to be put in a strait-jacket. His was a case of unrequited love as well. There was also the member of the cast who chained himself to the railings of the municipal library, though this was exhibitionism and had nothing to do with his heart. Years later he was in a 'live' play on television in which he had to crawl along a tube tunnel. He had quite a big part and died in the middle and never came out the other side.

I too was in love, with an actor who had remained with the company and who had once offered to buy me a winter coat. I had foolishly boasted of this proof of affection to my fellow detainees under the Tay Bridge and was immediately ordered to ask for the money rather than the garment itself. Three nights in succession I was sent out on to the mud-flats in a howling gale wearing nothing more than a threadbare cardigan in order to shiver more pathetically, but returned empty-handed. I can't remember how in the end we got enough money to return to London but I do know that we were all very weak and could have done with the leading lady to carry the luggage.

I was a lapsed Catholic long before I went to the altar, and even there I was not in a state of grace. The day before I was married my mother insisted that I go to the hairdresser's for a shampoo and set. Afterwards I had intended to make my confession to a local priest who had converted Wilfred Pickles. I so hated the look of my head that I ducked it in a puddle on the way to the church, and was then so appalled at what my mother would say – I was more scared of her than of God – that I spent an hour in the waiting room at the station trying to coax the curls back, and so missed confession altogether. Strictly speaking, my marriage the following day was invalid.

*

Martin Powell, his wife Rosie and their little son Jesse live not far from Christine and Patrick. When I went to their house Rosie was upstairs with Jesse. He's teething and she was trying to get him off to sleep.

Martin hadn't meant to live quite so close to his parents,

but the house came onto the market and it was too good a bargain to miss. They're still in the middle of doing it up, which is difficult because he, like Bruce, commutes every day to his accountancy job in the city and that doesn't leave much time for decorating – or for anything else for that matter. He'd like to join more in the life of the village. He goes to church on Sunday, and he manages the odd game of Eton Fives at Wokingham, but the rest of the weekend there's the house to see to, and of course he likes to spend as much time as possible with Rosie and Jesse.

He had been brought up, both at home and at school, to believe that helping one's community was important. His parents were on all sorts of committees. Christine worked for the Red Cross and the Old People's Club and the WI, and Patrick was a member of the Parish Council and on the governing board of the Treloar Trust which ran Treloar College for the handicapped. He was also still very active in the Worshipful Company of Haberdashers, of which he had been a Master. They weren't playing at being good. They worked extremely hard, writing letters, raising funds, arranging outings. It was something you did if you were lucky enough to be privileged; it was a way of giving something back in return.

When he'd left school he hadn't gone up to Cambridge like his father or his brother; instead he had studied languages at Heidelberg. He had intended to do something in the interpreting line, but he had realised that the sort of person who excelled at that sort of thing was very confident and go-ahead. He wasn't that sort of person. Passing exams hadn't come easily to him, unlike Bruce who sailed through most things. He'd enjoyed school when he was older, but he was quite unhappy at the beginning. Being sent away wasn't a question of wondering whether one's parents loved one, but rather whether anybody did.

Rosie, he said, hadn't gone to boarding school. She had been born in Belfast and attended grammar school in Derry.

Later her family moved to Australia and she went to sixth-form college there. She got a place at Aberystwyth University and had intended to do politics and librarianship, and she had qualified, but she hadn't enjoyed it as much as she had hoped. Having Jesse had been a shock to her – the dedication needed, the constant care and attention a child required. Even if they could afford it she wouldn't want a nanny. She believes very strongly that a child needs its own mother to take care of it. Why have one otherwise? All the same, the influence a mother has, the power she has to mould another human being, is a terrible responsibility. And nobody's ever given instruction on how to do it properly. It upsets her when she's out shopping and she hears the way some women shout at their small children, the kind of wounding sarcasm they use, the damaging words employed. She doesn't have any hard or fast rules, and she doesn't pretend to know the answers, but she wants Jesse to have confidence, something that she feels she herself had lacked.

They were giving a lot of thought to Jesse's education, even at this early stage. He'd go to the village school at first, and then at eleven or twelve, if he seemed secure and happy, they might send him away to board – but only if he was likely to benefit from it.

It wasn't a question of privilege or tradition, it was just that Martin himself had been well educated and it was natural to want his son to have the same chances. If they had a daughter, he wouldn't like to think he'd apply double standards. 'At least I hope I wouldn't,' he said. 'I wouldn't like to think I'd treat a daughter differently from a son.'

Religion was important to him; it sustained him when he felt sad. He'd been very fortunate, having such good parents, having had such a sound education, and of course he'd been more than fortunate to meet Rosie. She was good for him; she took him out of himself. She used to laugh at the way he folded up his clothes so neatly. She was his best friend.

*

Whenever I go back to Formby, the Lancashire village in which I grew up, I find in it nothing that reminds me of the past. It's become a dormitory town of Waterloo and Seaforth and Bootle. People who still live there assure me that it's exactly the same sort of place as it used to be, even if it seems different. All I know is that the war memorial at the end of the High Street looks smaller and less important, that there are two supermarkets, and that a housing estate covers those marshy fields which stretched to the pinewoods and the sea. The same, to an even greater extent, seeing that it is in the Home Counties, must be true of Bentley. The growing of hops and the hop-picking season is now but a small affair, and those laborious and frugal villagers, once sentimentally regarded as the yeomen of England – those hedge-trimmers and beekeepers, smiths and thatchers – are a dying breed. The country pubs, decorated with horse brasses and prints of hunting scenes, are full of weekend residents eating scampi out of little baskets, of shooting parties of city men ploughing their way through ploughman's lunches and merrily passing the sloe gin. Outside, large enough to accommodate both children and labradors, the estate cars choke the lanes. And yet, some things remain: the ordered fields, the oak trees and the pond, the black avenue of propped-up yews, five hundred years old, which leads to the door of St Mary's church, along which in the bitter-sweet past the Rev. Henry Austen, Curate of Bentley, escorted his sister Jane.

All the time I was with Patrick I had to keep remembering he had been a member of the Stock Exchange. I had visited the place once and a young man wearing a pin-stripe suit and holding a walkie-talkie to his ear had tried to explain to me what was agitating that throng who swarmed below us buzzing like worker bees. 'Most markets,' he had told me, 'deal in goods that have a practical use – the producers on the one hand providing a steady supply of goods, and the consumer, on the other, providing a steady demand. The Exchange deals in a different sort of commodity. The goods on sale, in themselves, have no intrinsic value. Stock and share certificates are merely evidence of a stake in a company, or, as in the case of Gilts, that money has been lent to the government by buying government stock.' He had added, rather honestly I thought, that share certificates and the like, though important documents which should be filed carefully, were of no 'use' whatsoever, not in the general meaning of the word. He went on to dazzle me with talk of Futures and Unit Trusts, Redemption Dates and Traded Options. I listened and marvelled, hypnotised by the poetical terms, by his baby cheeks quivering with importance, his innocent eyes shiny with percentages. Though he gave the illusion of running rings round himself he was only a little boy.

I was too polite to tell him that what he was saying was to me as scandalous as a lecture on the desirability of anti-semitism. God knows where it comes from, this illogical and wholly emotional reaction to stocks and shares, but it is a fact that if I was asked to spit on the flag or give away secrets I would do so without a qualm, but if my signature was required on a piece of paper which made me the purchaser of stocks and shares I would throw my pencil at the wall and hold out my hands for the thumbscrews. Such a puritanical and absurd response is possibly the fault of my father, that muddled man who voted Labour and yet was in business for himself, who detested the rich and yet whose sense of thrift drove him every night to empty the loose change from his pockets, sending the copper coins spinning across the brass tray on the Indian table beside the wardrobe, and who every morning without fail shovelled them into cotton bags and stored them in the ammunition tin he kept beneath the frilly valance of his single, lonely bed. Or perhaps I was influenced by Mrs Criddle and her Bevan boys, or by the *Ragged Trousered Philanthropists*. Most probably it has to do with Ernie Lambert.

On a Saturday my mother and father would drive in the car to Southport for afternoon tea and a visit to the first house of the pictures. It was in Southport that I became infatuated with Charles Boyer and saw the paintings of Fra Filippo Lippi. Worse, I met Minnie Lambert, who in her fox fur and her diamond earrings sat at a table nearest the potted palm in Thom's tea-shop. Minnie Lambert was rich. Her money came from Ernie, who was in Walton Jail, and nobody could understand how she could show her face after what had happened. My mother was friendly with her in a condescending sort of way. My father sat sideways from her, averting his eyes, and read his newspaper. Ernie was an embezzler and was in prison for seven years. He was well past middle-age and doubtless he would never come out; the shock of being locked up after living off the fat of the land would surely do for him. Once, when I asked what embezzlement entailed, my father launched into a tirade about stocks and shares and immorality and exploitation, and how come the revolution the Stock Exchange would be swept away. He implied that stocks and shares were drops of blood squeezed from the suffering masses of India and Africa, and that Ernie Lambert was no better than a Simon Legree. My mother just said it was a crying disgrace that Mrs Lambert still managed to buy her hats at the Bon Marché, and why hadn't the authorities confiscated her fox fur and her jewels long ago. Looking back, I feel sorry for Minnie; the last thing she needed while she buttered her muffins was my mother, and yet I know how my mother must have felt too – all her life spent making ends meet because such dishonesties were out of her range, and at the end of it all, in spite of the law, the stigma, the shame, Minnie Lambert in full view, bold as brass, tinkling her charm bracelet above the electroplated teapot.

*

Patrick told me that he didn't mind being old, not so long as he had Christine with him. They liked listening to music, and travelling, and of course they were both passionate gardeners. He didn't say so, but I imagine he couldn't live anywhere else but in the country. He wouldn't have fitted in in the city. It simply wasn't his style to go to dinners or operas or clubs. He would have thought it a foolish way to spend his time. He belonged to the old school, to the old England. A village is surely the only place left where a man of substance, of some wealth, can lead a Christian life.

We were in the garden again – Christine and Patrick were raking up leaves for a bonfire – waiting for the rest of the family to come to tea. Martin and Rosie had already arrived; they were doing something to the apple trees in the orchard. Jesse was standing in the avenue of box hedges, mesmerised by the sunlight flashing from a spider's web.

We talked about England, about the possible differences between North and South. Christine said that during the war they had p.g'd with some lovely people in Yorkshire. 'They were very kind, very sweet, they couldn't have made us feel more welcome. It was just after the Battle of Britain and anyone in an RAF uniform was treated wonderfully. I don't think it would have been the same in the South.'

'Perhaps not,' said Patrick. 'But things have changed everywhere since then. There's much more equality now.'

'Much more,' agreed Christine.

'It's more difficult for the employer now,' said Patrick. 'The employee doesn't bow down in obedience any more. If he's asked to do something, he wants to know the reason why, and quite right too, but in the past when he was asked to do something he just got on with it, like the thin red line at Balaclava. Ours but to do or die and all that.'

If I was ever going to ask the Powells about money, about

the unfairness of those who have and those who haven't, now was the time. 'Do you think money brings responsibilities?' I began.

'Oh, but of course,' said Patrick. 'It's tremendously important to realise the value of it, to understand that it shouldn't be frittered away. The wrong usage of wealth can be every bit as damaging to the individual as the lack of it. My father taught me that. He was prepared to make sacrifices to give me a good education. Do you know, I can remember him every night emptying his pockets and saving his loose change. I've always done exactly the same myself.'

Bruce and Lizzie's children arrived and danced among the leaves. Patrick had set a barrel on the grass with a plank across it for his grandchildren to use as a see-saw. Then it came to me, that forgotten memory of another garden in which I had walked with my father. Only a small one after all, behind a suburban house, but on just such a day, the grass fading and the trees growing bare. 'Rabbits,' he had said, 'eat every blasted thing in sight and have no conception of tomorrow.' And it came to me also that my father's attitudes, his fear, his thrift, his belief in education, his prejudices, were not dissimilar to those of the Powells, and that the differences between classes, between regions, were as nothing when compared with the differences between generations.

5

The Johnsons of Northumberland

It seemed to take for ever, those last five miles to Ossie Johnson's farm, Ottercops, up into the hills with the moorland stretching on either side and the trees all bent against the wind. There was a row of rats pegged out like stiff rags on the wire above the ditch beside the road. We were in Northumberland, a region haunted by death, bounded in the west by the Cheviot Hills, divided from the south by distance and from Scotland by an ancient and blood-soaked border. Carrion crows burst from a black copse as a Harrier jet blasted out of the piled up clouds.

The Johnsons live in a grey rendered farmhouse surrounded by a cluster of pens and outhouses. There were hens in the yard, pecking in the mud ruts, and a rooster stalking the wall. An older, original farmhouse, its roof green with moss, stood in a hollow beyond the fence. There was an intermittent wailing, like the crying of newborn babies in a maternity ward, coming from an open-ended barn behind the house. Something large panted inside a stone lean-to.

Ossie and Margaret were having breakfast. From the kitchen window Margaret looks out on nothing but fields and sky. The sky was twice as vast as the land.

'We don't want a nuclear power station in Northumberland, thank you very much,' said Ossie, responding to an item in his newspaper.

'Eat your breakfast, my dear,' said Margaret, putting a plate of bacon and eggs in front of him.

'I'm dressing lambs today,' Ossie told her. 'There'll be half a dozen men extra for dinner, if you would be so kind as to feed them.'

'Mmmm,' said Margaret.

Ossie was named after Oswald, a Northumbrian king.

131

He's a tenant farmer with 1053 hectares of land on which he husbands two thousand sheep. He's passionate about his flock. He says that sheep are in his blood and that he thinks of himself as one of the black-faced breeders' clan. For generations his family worked the land, first as border raiders, then as sheep stealers, and eventually as farmers. His father owned a small-holding in Cumberland and moved to Northumberland before the war. He took a tenancy at Ferneyrigg, Kirkwhelphinton, a farm which is still managed by one son, Jacob. Ossie married Margaret Cleghorn, a music teacher, in 1952. She is the daughter of a farm-worker who lived at Wallington Hall, an eighteenth-century house belonging to the Trevelyan shipping family. She's a student of natural history, of graveyards, a botanist, a photographer, a map-maker, a woman of varied interests and curiosity who doesn't much care for cooking and who spends most of her time at the stove. Men who shepherd sheep have to be well fed; a countryman's strength, both of body and spirit, is his greatest asset, for he must last the toiling day and accept with patience the capricious moods of a natural world. Though sometimes she may feel that she is wasted, particularly when the goat has just eaten her geraniums, Margaret appreciates the results of her labour.

'I'm always glad I married a farmer 'cos they've got muscles. They've got muscular bodies and muscular arms. I don't like townspeople with soft hands. Young people today, well some young people, they've got soft bellies and flabby arms. I don't like men with soft white hands. I like farmers because they're men. Farmers look weatherbeaten. And they behave like men. It's just like Ossie – up here in the hills we have crisis after crisis, what with the weather and things, and he just goes doggedly on. And you have to make your own decisions. There's no time to consult with anyone else. It could make you very self-opinionated, this sort of life. If you were in the South you wouldn't need to be so determined, so dogged.'

'Does that mean you'd have been a different person if you'd been born somewhere else?' I asked.

'Now would I?' pondered Margaret. 'No, I can't say I would. People, as such, aren't different. It's not where you come from but how much money you have. People are very commercial these days. The young are more classless, because they go to university and they mix more – but it's when you get into the suburbs when people feel they have to be something that you find the classes forming. I dare say I'd feel different down there. If I cross a certain line in the country, if I go South, I do feel more mellow. For one thing I don't have to wear woollens. Southerners don't have to fight the weather. Up here the springs are late and very cold, especially these last three years, and you just have to stick it out.'

Ossie had gone out to the barn to his sheep. Earlier they had been driven down from the hills to be dipped, rounded up by men on ponies as though it was the Wild West. I'd always thought that sheep wandered about on their own, cropping grass and dropping lambs in the snow. I hadn't realised that they have to be shepherded twice a day – in the morning brought down to the sweeter grass and in the evening pushed back up again into the hills.

Sheep have to be watched because of the foxes in the forests and the carrion crows which can peck out the eyes of a newborn lamb. And they have to be 'looked' at in case they fall on to their backs; sheep, like turtles, can't right themselves on their own. In olden times shepherds were like priests, celibate through circumstances and living their lives in solitude, contemplating nature and guarding their flocks. The crook is the same as the bishop's crozier. An ancient custom buried the shepherd with a staple of wool so that come Judgement Day he'd have his excuse for not having attended church on Sunday. It's very biblical, this shepherding business. When he dipped his sheep – standing in a sort of watch tower above a moat, dunking his lambs under the disinfectant with a yard brush – Ossie must have felt a bit like John the Baptist, except that *his* followers had leapt joyfully into the waters of the Jordan to be washed of their sins and the sheep had been less than willing to be rid of their ticks. That's where Ossie's muscles had come in useful. A man has to have strength in his arms to purify his flock.

Ossie was now dressing his animals, preparing them for the Bellingham Fair in a week's time. He was cutting the ruff away from their necks so that they would hold their heads up more proudly and shearing the tangled wool from their hindquarters. He gripped each animal between his thighs as though he was playing the cello. His son-in-law Bruce was helping him. Brenda, his daughter, was leaning over the pen, watching. Ossie wouldn't let her help. She's pregnant and a struggling sheep has a kick like a mule.

'There are three things we have to do with sheep,' Ossie said, 'and I dare say with anything else – breed them as best as you know how, farm them as well as you are able, and sell them as profitably as you can. I sell my mule lambs for breeding in the lowlands.'

'Mules,' I said.

'Aye,' he said. 'And there's gimmers and wethers, that is lambs that have had a first shearing and ones that have been castrated. And then there's tups, they're males, and hogs, which are female breeders. Tups are mules.'

I would have liked to have known which ones were Sunday joints, but for all I knew Ossie's sheep never saw the inside of an oven so I asked instead if they ever slept. I'd never seen a sleeping sheep.

'I've come across a yow,' he said, 'and I thought it was dead. And I prodded it and it was just slumbering.'

'A yow?'

'It's my way of saying ewe,' he explained.

'They're not stupid, are they?' I said.

'Not as stupid as people,' he agreed. 'Or as cows. My word, no.'

We talked about his children. He has four. Two daughters are married to farmers and the third to an engineer. 'My son Roly,' he said, 'tried farming and he decided it wasn't on. If a young man doesn't like farming or sheep, then it's just one of those things. There's a great lack of common sense these days, and there's a great many openings in the world. If a young man uses his common sense, that's the main thing. There's more freedom than in my day and some things have changed, but the principles remain the same. The Christian experience is the most important experience in life. After all, David was a shepherd and he defended his sheep against the lions and against all comers, and Jesus was a great shepherd and still is, you know, and he loves them now as much as he did then.'

'Yes,' I said, there not being much else I could reply to that.

'It's easier in the countryside to be a Christian,' he continued. 'In the city there's temptation round every corner. Up here in the hills, among the sheep, you're a bit nearer to heaven, I believe. But sheep runs in families. You're either a sheep man or you're not.'

I asked who in his family, apart from himself, had sheep in their blood, and he indicated with his scissors his red-headed daughter, Brenda.

Brenda and her husband Bruce Walton farm Todholes in Elsdon. Unlike her brother and sisters who boarded she attended school locally and then went on to agricultural college. Bruce is an auctioneer and she met him at a Young Conservatives dance. She never wanted to be anything else but a farmer. She was milking Daisy, the cow, when I went to visit her, filling a pail to feed a litter of collie pups.

'I liked music and art at school, but I knew I'd be a farmer. The teachers didn't like it. Nobody really wants girls on farms unless it's to do the cooking, and I wanted to really farm, to learn all about sheep. It's not that men don't think you're equal, it's more that it's so hard physically. Up on a hill-farm it's like there's a battle going on all the time between the land and you, and it never ends and you can't ever turn your back on it. We manage cows here as well as sheep, but I prefer the sheep. It's hard to explain. You have to have it in the blood to know what I mean.'

She said her mother didn't have the same feeling for animals, not to that extent, but she had a great feel for the land. When they were all children she used to take them on picnics and tell them about history and wild flowers and rock formations.

'My mother knows about history. And about music. We've all inherited this ability for music. Kathie – she's married to a farmer – she studied at Newcastle and she runs two Sunday music groups. Christine trained as a nurse but gave it up. For a time she got involved with gospel singers and then later she went to music college. She's got pure talent. Kathie has to work hard and is very good but Chris is the natural. She sings in the Methodist church choir. You'll meet them this morning.'

'I would have liked to be able to play an instrument,' I said. 'I don't know a thing about music, just that it sounds good and makes me go off into daydreams.'

'It's more of a curse being musical, than anything else,' said Brenda, pushing her head against Daisy's flank. They both had red hair though Brenda's was lighter, more fiery in tone.

'If you want to do music properly,' she said, 'you have to practise and you can't do much of that if you're a farmer. And there's the temperament that goes with it, the moods. Artistic people may be more colourful as characters, but, oh, the swings of mood that accompany it. It's not comfortable.'

We took the milk to the puppies who were locked in a shed with their mother. They ran round our ankles and fell over in the mud. The wind was blowing the rain across the yard. I asked Brenda when her baby was expected and she told me, and then she said it was her second child. Her first,

Richard Walton, had died a cot-death last year. She had gone into his room at seven o'clock in the morning and looked down at him and known that he was gone. Believing in God had helped, and now, of course, there was the joy of the new baby to come.

We shut the puppies away and went inside to have a cup of tea. There was a photograph in a frame of Richard in his coffin. I was glad to be inside out of the wind; Brenda gazed out of the window at the damp meadow behind the house and the rough stone wall which divided it from the fields and the distant, grazing sheep.

'When you leave agricultural school,' she said, 'you're outside all the time, just like the men, and then when you get married – I've been married three years – you realise that a farmer's wife spends most of her time in the kitchen. When I first realised that it was terrible, I can tell you. I like being out there. There's something about living on the land which is bigger, deeper than just being fond of animals. I think even Roly liked that part of it. But it's more than that.'

Kathie and Christine, her two older sisters, arrived. Kath has a little son and daughter and Christine has three children, Kirsty, Steven and Stuart. Kath is a farmer's wife. Bill, Chris's husband, is unemployed. His being at home has its advantages as well as its disadvantages. Chris always has someone to keep an eye on the children but then he's always under her feet. Kath is small and dark and Chris is tall with melancholy eyes.

I told them we'd been talking about Roly.

'Oh, Roly,' said Kath, and smiled.

'He's happier in himself now,' Brenda said. 'Now that he's left the farm. He did try to have a go at it, he did try to be the traditional farmer's son but his heart wasn't in it.'

Kathie said; 'You have to have it in you to be a hill-farmer ... because it's all to do with stock breeding; it's not like crops. We haven't the weather for crops, and knowing about stock is a special thing. You either feel it or you don't. I think our Dad secretly still minds that Roly couldn't make a go of it.'

'Well, he minded at first,' agreed Brenda, 'but he wants the best for Roly. All farmers mind if their sons go off, especially if it's to do with music, and pop at that. People round here are very conservative in their ways and when they heard Roly had gone off to be a pop-star they thought he'd gone off his head.'

'They're very clannish in Elsdon,' Kath said. 'Clannish but honest.'

'They're nosey round Corbridge,' said Chris. 'Bill got a job, only a couple of days' work, and someone told on him.'

'It's expensive now,' said Kath, 'to employ people. There's a lot of unemployment and snoopers are always reporting moonlighters to the DHSS.'

'They're drinkers in the Rede valley,' Brenda told me. 'You can go from one area to another and the people are different in outlook. You wouldn't think it possible.'

I tried to get them to talk about childhood. I said how wonderful it must have been to grow up on a farm. I was thinking of log fires and motherless lambs and a kitchen fragant with the smell of new-baked bread.

'Thinking back on it it was wonderful,' agreed Kath.

'It was,' Chris said. 'But then we were sent away to school.'

'Our mother was always taking us on picnics to the sea,' said Kathie. 'With Nan and Grandad Cleghorn.'

'I didn't like going away to school,' Chris said.

I wondered if for all of them their childhood had been so encompassing, so bright, that nothing afterwards had matched up to it and that all their lives they'd feel they'd been pushed out of the garden of Eden.

Kath remembered that their father had never gone on picnics with them, only her mother and grandparents. At the time she had accepted it. Now that she has children and she too takes them off on their own, she thinks about it more.

But it was a wonderful childhood.

'You wanted to learn dancing,' said Chris. 'And you couldn't because there weren't any teachers.'

I asked if Roly had helped in the house when he was a boy.

'He tried everything to get out of the washing up,' said Kathie. 'You know, he'd fall on the floor and pretend to collapse, but we used to pull him up, drag him up. We wouldn't let him get away with it.'

'He could iron,' Brenda said. 'And make jam tarts.'

I wanted to know if the sisters were close, if they saw a lot of each other. Chris said that she and Kath were especially friendly. They had deep conversations about the Christian faith. But then, they were all religious. Even Roly.

'You know what lads ... what men are like,' said Kath. 'Pretending to be superindependent – I can manage on me own, I don't need help – that sort of thing. But deep down he believes. He just hasn't gone as far along the road as we have.'

I went to see Roly the following day. He lives with his wife Liz in a terraced house in Newcastle. He's trying to make his way as a composer and performer of popular songs. He had only just returned from his honeymoon. It's only twenty miles from Ottercops to Newcastle, yet the distance he has travelled in defecting to the city is hard to calculate. He's tall and has the same large eyes as his mother and her direct manner of speech. In a corner of the small living-room was a glittering amplifier and a set of drums. On the wall above the fireplace hung a framed photograph of his uncle wearing a trilby hat, squatting on his haunches cheek to cheek with a haughty looking sheep.

'It would have been handy,' Roly said, 'if I'd had a brother. Then I wouldn't have felt an obligation to stay on the farm. I still do farm work from time to time. I was shearing up at Otterburn this morning. But I'm a very bad shepherd – I tend to look at the clock. I used to go round in a

139

Land Rover ... well, it was always raining ... and I needed a cup of coffee every hour or so. I never got any satisfaction out of it. The others, they never seemed to notice the time, they could spend all day at it, out there in all weathers. They got a sort of enjoyment out of it. Me, I never even got close to it. It might seem a bit foolish, giving up a ready-made living, but I've got too many interests to stay in one place. I want to try and make a go of the music.'

'Townfolk,' I said, 'think of life on a farm as paradise. Man pitting himself against the elements and all that.'

'That's as may be,' he said. 'Before we moved here we lived in the old farmhouse at Ottercops. It was so damp the water was running down the walls. All we pitted ourselves against was pneumonia.'

*

My brother wanted to be a farmer though my mother had marked him down as a lawyer. He flunked Latin twice but she drove him on. She considered labouring in the fields, unless you were a land-owner, a menial occupation. Why, Tommy Sutton was a farmer, and he delivered the milk in a horse-drawn cart and never wore a pair of trousers that wasn't patterned with cow-dung. Jimmy Bennett was a farmer, sort of, and he had got drunk one August Bank Holiday and beaten his wife over the head with a dead rabbit. It was brains that were needed to get on in life, not brawn. It was true that farmers didn't quite fit into the category of the working-class, but that was only because they lived in old houses and drove tractors and had an unusual relationship with crops and animals and the seasons. According to my mother, farmers were a class apart and best left that way. And yet it was her fault that my brother yearned to be one.

My grandfather had been a director of Goodlass Walls, a paint firm in Liverpool. He had an interest in a barytes mine near Welshpool in Shropshire. God knows what barytes did, though somewhere along the line it got put into gallons of paint. When she was a little girl my mother went down the mine in a tin hat with a candle fixed to the front. She said it was warm under the earth. Often in dreams I see her floating moth-pale – she's always wearing a white dress – flickering in candlelight along those propped-up passageways, hand in hand with her father.

When he was on mine business my grandfather stayed at the Herbert Arms Hotel in Chirbury. It was more of a public house with accommodation for paying guests than an hotel, but my mother grew so attached to the neighbourhood and had such happy memories of the past that when she was grown and married she brought her children there for the holidays.

We went to Chirbury because we needed a break from Formby where we lived. A change of scene was as good as a tonic, and Shropshire, being so far from Lancashire, was a foreign country. The people spoke with strange tongues and even the vegetables tasted different. As for the air, we slept like tops and ate like turkey cocks.

In the beginning the Herbert Arms was an inn, and then later an L-shaped dining-room was tacked to the side. The house fronted directly onto the road. This was handy for my father, who on numerous occasions, spotting his detested father-in-law in the doorway, hand raised in welcome, would bring the car screeching to a halt within a yard of our destination; leaping out he would manhandle the trunk free from the washing-line that bound it to the lid of the boot and dump it on the cobblestones, urging us in the choicest of sentences to follow, and when at last we were all out, standing there as though struck by lightning, clutching our teddies and our fishing nets, he would fling himself back into the driving seat and reversing, roar off in the direction from which we had come like a man leaving a sinking ship.

Next door, separated from the Herbert Arms by a high

141

wall, lived Albert Jones. He was an unremarkable man, until in the last year of the war he was flung over in love by a land girl from Chester. Losing his mind, he ran to his bedroom overlooking the graveyard and all day long blasted his rabbit gun at the tombstones, the village bobby and my Uncle Charlie, wearing bin-lids, entreating him to come down and go quietly.

Round the corner was the village shop on the little road to Marton and the Sun Inn managed by Auntie Belle. The shop was owned by Charlie Davies who made sheep's eyes at my Auntie Lily. Auntie Belle was sister to Auntie White, wife of Uncle Charlie who was the proprietor of the Herbert Arms. None of them, Belle or Charlie or Auntie White, were related to us, but my mother was devoted to them. Charlie had once worked in the potteries, painting roses on plates and vases. Auntie White had a wall-eye and spent all her time cooking. They were happily married, which was a condition I had not often encountered, and once, seeing them in bed together, Auntie White with her hair in plaits and Uncle Charlie in a night-cap, propped up on pillows drinking tea, I ran away down the stairs and hid in the cow-shed. To me, as a child, they were both in that middle age in which each had a foot in the grave, and yet something in that glimpse of them through the parted curtain of their landing bedroom alarmed me. I had never seen anything so friendly, so intimate.

The hotel had a staff of three, a land girl named Sybil – the same one who drove Albert out of his wits – Mrs Parry the cleaning lady and Fred the cowman who bothered me. When I was little Fred used to come into my room to kiss me goodnight. One evening I locked the door before he came up the stairs, and fell asleep. My mother, finding the room shut tight, called my Uncle Charlie who fetched a ladder to the front of the house and climbed through the window. I couldn't explain why I had locked myself in. I said that I was scared of ghosts and everyone said that I was at the age for it.

Behind the hotel lay the yard with its manure heap, the

cowsheds, the pigsties and the hay barn. All night long there was a clinking of chains as the cows shifted in their stalls. When the pub closed the men came out and relieved themselves against the wall, and if it was Christmas and the nights were full of frost, you could hear the water splattering against the stones, rattling like breaking glass. Sometimes a farm labourer, too inebriated to mount his bike and ride the dark lanes, would go through into the scullery and climb the steps to the loft to sleep it off, lying down in the straw beneath the rafters hung with sides of bacon white in the moonlight, the salt-crusted hanks glistening like melting snow.

The guests who came to stay at the hotel were mainly women who were touched by tragedy. Mrs Hargreaves' husband had been blown to pieces in Burma; Elsie Dobbins' sweetheart was missing over Frankfurt. The husband of Mrs Rimmer's niece had had his face burned away in a tank in the desert. Mrs Rimmer's George had been torpedoed. Auntie Belle at Marton was one of the lucky ones. Her son had been shot down over enemy territory and had made his way back across the mountains and frontiers of occupied Europe to fly again.

Once, we all went on a walk together, my Auntie Lily, whose husband was in a reserved occupation, Mrs Rimmer, Mrs Hargreaves, Elsie Dobbins, my mother and myself. We went along the path beside Harrington Hall, a home for naughty boys. They had all come from rich families and had been to public schools, which was why my mother referred to them as sad cases rather than as criminals. The path led beside a trickling stream and the dammed-up pool, cold as cold, in which in high summer we splashed shrieking in shaded sunlight, and rose up through tangled trees to the sky. It was a long walk, and we chatted all the way up and nobody told me to keep quiet. Elsie Dobbins played the mouth organ. You couldn't tell what tune it was because she was so breathless. At the top we all rested and drank lemonade brought by Mrs Hargreaves in her haversack. Below us we could see the church tower through the trees, and a little black car winding its way on black market petrol up the hill to Corndon. Elsie Dobbins lay on her back and watched the sky as though looking for that missing aeroplane.

When it was time to go home I said we should go straight down and not bother with the path. It would be quicker and more of an adventure. I didn't expect them to take any notice and I was quite looking forward to slithering down on my own and reaching the stream before anybody else. As I rule I travelled with Charles Boyer and other people were a crowd. But for some reason my mother thought it was a good idea, and so did Auntie Lily. In no time at all they were bounding and rolling down the hill, buffeted by trees and clawed at by bushes. Mrs Hargreaves, who detested litter-bugs, jettisoned her lemonade bottle. Mrs Rimmer caught her stocking on a blackberry bramble and acted as though she had severed a main artery. My mother swore a lot and threatened to break my neck if ever we reached the bottom alive. We were pursued by midges and stung by nettles as we broke through spiders' webs slung like blobs of jelly between the branches. They all put up a terrible caterwauling, that Greek chorus of war widows, shouting and screaming hysterically, and when we did reach the stream my mother and Elsie Dobbins had to make a chair of their linked hands to carry Auntie Lily to the telephone box on the Marton road. She said her ankle was sprained. Uncle Charlie came in his car to take them home. Mrs Hargreaves said I was a candidate for Harrington Hall. To be fair, my mother didn't shout at me, she just wouldn't speak to me.

There were eight cows in the yard, and it was my brother's job to milk them and muck out the shed. He would get up at five in the morning to herd them down the yard and out into the lane, clattering like tap-dancers as they slipped on the cobbles, past the village shop and up the road to the fields.

Often he would take his supper into the shed and squat on the stone floor, his back to the dung-flecked wall, eating by lantern light. I begged him to give me a turn, to lend me the thin stick he kept propped up behind the milk churns and drive the cows all on my own to the meadow, but he wouldn't hear of it. He said it was his job and I was to get lost. I used to spy on him from the bushes and I couldn't understand the expression on his face – that mysterious half smile he wore as though he was just on the point of understanding some secret joke – as he strolled through the morning light swishing the hedgerows with his stick. I realise now that he must have had cows in his blood.

One afternoon, as he was in the shed preparing to loosen the chains, I asked again if I could have a turn, and this time he said, 'Shut up, face-ache.' I picked up the mucking-out brush – it was so heavy I had to use both hands – and I swung it up like a croquet mallet and brought it down on his head. He still smiled for a moment, as if he'd felt nothing, and then he fell down.

They were all against me. They said I was spoilt and uncontrolled. I was sent to bed and I started coughing, great whoops that could be heard in the dining-room. They said I was putting it on, which I was. My brother didn't need stitches or anything. He just had a bump like a doorhandle above his left ear. I spent most of the rest of that holiday in the outside privy in the kitchen garden across the road. It was my little house. I could hear them talking in the pavilion and hear the click of the bowls as they rolled church bias across the green. I read the *Girls Crystal* magazine from cover to cover, sitting on the floor with the sunlight running like coloured beads along the cracks in the wooden roof.

My brother never did become a farmer. Instead he set himself up as a country solicitor in Montgomeryshire, three miles from the Herbert Arms Hotel, and brought himself a Hall with a river running through the boundary of his fields.

*

Brenda took me in the Land Rover to a beagle meet in the grounds of Little Harle Tower, a country residence which was a cross between a house and a castle. It had stone urns on the steps and walls covered with scarlet creeper. We stood on the lawn surrounded by people drinking sherry out of paper cups, and then the Master of the Hunt said how kind it was of John and Kitty to allow us the use of their grounds, and that he was sure we'd all have a happy day. I wasn't so confident. Nobody had offered me a drink; I think they mistook me for one of those animal rights campaigners.

The huntsman, Nigel, the fellow who leads the pack, was a milkman from Gloucestershire. You're not allowed to call his animals dogs; they're hounds. And they don't have tails, just sterns. Nigel was wearing white breeches and a black riding hat and looked very smart. Some were in red waistcoats and tweed britches. The rest of us wore a uniform of green anoraks and green wellies. The capacity of the English, of whatever class, to indulge in sport, of whatever kind, is only equalled by their genius for dressing the part.

I was amazed, when everything got under way, to see the undignified scramble for cars. The huntsman ran ahead with his hounds and we followed on wheels until we came out of the drive and into open country. Then we left the cars and trotted, binoculars bouncing about our chests, in a business-like fashion along the hedgerows.

Almost at once a hare was flushed, and the 'Gone Away' call was blown on the horn. I could see the hare, we all could, running almost leisurely across the grass higher up the hill. The hounds were lower down, turning in circles and wagging their sterns. They don't chase by sight but by scent, and no amount of shouting and pointing in the right direction does any good, but then not being seen doesn't help the hare much either.

I could see the sense in beagling; it's very healthy, all that jogging about on foot in the open air and doubling back on one's tracks. Nigel looked splendid, cantering on shanks's pony in his romantic knickerbockers, his black acorn hat bobbing against the horizon as he breasted the hill. Three minutes later they blew the horn for the kill. It happened behind a clump of bushes – the death – and then the hounds were off again on a new scent. I couldn't understand why people kept falling to the earth as though struck by some deadly virus, until it was explained to me that if you happen to be standing, gawking, when the hare leaps past, you have to bob down out of sight. I hoped it had something to do with Christian reticence but I suspected it had more to do with shape, with subtle gradation of light and the fact that hares can see sideways and behind but not straight ahead. It could explain the zigzag course they took, dodging the rolling shadows that swept across the hills as the sun played hide and seek with the clouds.

Those who see an anachronism in a mechanised and overfed society hunting the fields on horse or foot should remember that the chase is only a small part of a lost and profounder way of life, a last link with a rural England that has all but disappeared.

At the close of the day, though I didn't stay to hear it, the horn blew 'Going Home', a melancholy penny-whistle scale of notes signalling retreat and the end of the hunt.

At night the beaglers gathered in the local hotel for a celebration dinner. They danced 'Strip the Willow' to a band led by a gentleman with a sticking plaster over one eyebrow. The hotel had booked two bands by mistake and it was rumoured that a fight had ensued to settle the issue. Lord Davenport, Ossie's landlord, was there, a young man who is a qualified architect and who studied at Newcastle University. His estate of thirteen thousand acres was given to him as a twenty-first birthday present. He travels a lot and has worked as an architect in Japan and Israel and New

York. He talked about the threat of forestation to hill farmers, the fact that you can get six times the capital return if you put trees on the land. The counter argument is that it's too much of a long-term gain because the capital lay-out is so great. His land is controlled by a trust, and so far he has resisted pressure to set aside more of the land for planting. Hundreds of years ago Arden and Sherwood, Dean and Epping still stood dark and of almost impenetrable thickness, though by Elizabeth I's reign the government were alarmed at the rate the trees were being felled for ship-building and for houses. In the North, which remained lawless far longer than the South, the forests continued to be used by outlaws and by robbers. And yet there were still more sheep in England than there were men and women. Lord Davenport likes Northumberland. In the South farmers are more like business men – here they have to work more closely with the land. It's a question of the weather. The people in the hills still accept an almost feudal system; sixty per cent of farmers are tenants. There's a difference between the profitable and intensive arable farming in the Lowlands and the tougher less rewarding farming of the hills, where the area is large but the cultivation small. That's why he's under such pressure to go all out for forestry. At the moment they're attempting a compromise, which is expensive but could justly be regarded as progress, though probably not by Ossie.

I went outside for a breath of air. There were wild clouds and a sickle moon curved like a hunting horn above the black spine of the hills.

*

Right up to the last minute Ossie titivated his sheep ready for the annual sale. He had washed their faces with soapy water and I shouldn't be surprised if he hadn't dabbed after-shave behind their ears. His mules were shown inside a circular building with a hole in the roof. When the class was called the boys opened the pens in the corral outside and the sheep flowed down the twisting corridors, entering on tiptoe like a *corps de ballet*, teetering first to one side and then the other, their golden eyes catching the light, red marks on their faces like lipstick kisses, blue indigo on their backs to signify their owners. The auctioneer raised his baton to begin the bidding, gabbling an incantation which rose and fell and rose again like a roll of drums, and the spectators on the tiered benches, those farmers from Stonefolds and Cranberry Brow, Chirdon, East Bog, Allenwash Fell, Goatstones and Redesmouth, Pondershaw and Soppit, marked their white papers above the sawdust ring and remained inscrutable. Ossie and Brenda were both there, dragging their long sticks across the sawdust as though persuading their flock to leap through hoops. This was the culmination of a year's hard work, all that husbanding and shepherding, that fighting of the good fight that never ends.

When it was over, Ossie pronounced himself satisfied. It had all been worthwhile, particularly this back end of the year. Even if it hadn't been he didn't see what else he could do. He wouldn't want to do anything else, grow corn or tatties in the Lowlands or that sort of thing. He just wanted to be with his sheep. 'Like them,' he said, 'I'm hefted to the hills.'

*

I had tea with Margaret. She had promised to show me her collection of pressed flowers. Outside in the evening light the thistle heads were gleaming like steel. Earlier she had been at Stamford village hall, accompanying her over-sixties choir on the piano. Most of them are women, of course. It's possible that some of the gentlemen had preferred to stay at home to watch television, but statistically it was more likely that the ladies were widows. They had sung 'Little Things

Mean a Lot', that melody whose words go: 'Give me your arm as we cross the street, give me your shoulder to cry on … Don't have to buy me diamond and pearls … rubies … sable and furs … honestly honey, they just mean money … '
They enjoy their choir. It's nice to know there's a club to come to, and songs of sentiment to be sung, recalling those younger days when eyes were bright and a shoulder to lean on was more essential than a stick. It's funny how Americans always go on about money. An Englishman would say a girl was as pretty as a picture; an American would tell her she looked like a million dollars.

Margaret has always been interested in plants, in dried petals and grasses. 'My family were all gardeners...my own family...the one I've got now … are anything but. When I was small, outdoor toilets were like little houses – I always put a jar of bluebells in ours. My mother used to laugh at me. I would have liked to have pursued botany but my family couldn't afford university and I went to training college instead and became a teacher. I've always been interested in rocks, and, of course, that leads on to plants. It tells you about history. Round here, the earth is full of the past. The land is steeped in blood. They did terrible things to one another. I've given up though on keeping a garden of my own. I just haven't the heart any more. I had two rhododendrons in tubs at the front, and Mandy the goat charged through the fence and tossed them about. There were just spikes left. Then I tried alpines, but she ate them as well. Later I grew some geraniums. I thought I'd enter them for the show. They were just coming into bloom, they were beautiful, and then Mandy gobbled them up. I'm sick of livestock. We had to have the vet to Mandy when she devoured the rhododendrons. They made her ill.'

'Serve her right,' I said.

'She recovered, but I've given up trying to grow anything. Ossie has put the sheep in the plot where I grew the flowers. Mandy suckles motherless lambs in there now.'

'You could try cacti,' I suggested.

'No,' said Margaret. 'I've given up. I can't go on. I've bought artificial flowers instead. You know, these days they make them so lifelike. I never thought it would come to that but it has.'

*

It was Harvest Festival and the Johnson family went to the Methodist church hall to sing their praises to God. Margaret played the piano. 'We plough the fields and scatter, the good seed on the land, but it is fed and watered by God's almighty hand.' The door was open, showing an oblong of sky and the sun splintering through the trees. It was easy, what with the music and the heady scent of flowers arranged on the trestle table, to sense the mystery of God blazing behind the seasons. All the same, I felt out of place, like a tourist. It seems to me that the gulf which exists between those who dwell on the land and those who live in cities has grown too wide to bridge, and that we are the ones who are crying in the wilderness. They're not perfect, these hill folk who tend sheep, but you could say they stand on a green platform between heaven and hell, those two regions the rest of us believe we only visit when alive.

6

The Roses of Birmingham

'Up to five years ago,' Debbie said, 'there were no coloured people in Quinton.'

'We'd get on the bus ...' began Judy.

'There was only the odd Paki shop,' said Debbie.

'And people would stare at us and say, hasn't he got a lovely suntan,' Judy said.

'I was taking Aaron into work,' Debbie explained. 'He was just born, and he was all in white and this woman kept looking at him, and she said, isn't he brown, isn't he brown, she just went on and on, and she was really white, and so I said, yes, we've just come back from France if you want to know. Because that's how I get.'

'Oh, she does,' said Judy.

'I don't have to explain what I do to anyone else. It's my business. I mean, that woman at the bus stop who kept staring. You'd think he had six heads ... I said, 'scuse me, can you see something I can't see?'

'She did,' said Judy. 'When I knew Debbie was pregnant, the first time, I didn't think, oooh it's black, I mean I just thought, oooh it's a baby. It could have been yellow, black or white. I think it's harder though having black children. I mean, people immediately ...'

'Assume,' said Debbie.

'Put a label on you. Think you're no good,' Judy said.

'We was never told,' said Debbie, 'not to mix with blacks, not to go out with them. When I was seventeen and I said I was going to Barbados with Mervyn, me Dad never knew he was black.'

'Mum did,' said Judy.

'And when I told him, I must admit he wasn't pleased. And then he said, all right, I better meet him. And when he met him he was great. He was great.'

'It wasn't that quick,' said Judy.

155

Harry and Nora Rose have five daughters: Diane, Judy, Beverley, Jackie and Debbie. They're a close family and the girls see each other almost every day. On a Saturday they all go to their Mum's for lunch. On Fridays, Debbie and Judy go into the centre of Birmingham and have breakfast at Littlewoods. It's their treat. On Wednesdays they take the children to Macdonald's for lunch. Afterwards they go round the dress shops.

Harry left school at fourteen, and when he was fifteen he chucked in his job as a teaboy at a pram-making firm and went on the halls. He toured all over England with Florrie Ford. His wife Nora was born in Birmingham, She lived four doors away from Harry. She left school at fourteen and worked in a shop until she had the children. Later she did part-time work as a cleaner. She gave that up two years ago because of emphysema. Harry has lived on the same estate for fifty years. He can remember when it was surrounded by fields. For the last ten years he's worked as a maintenance man for British Leyland. He sees the necessity for automation – to survive one has to have maximum efficiency. All the same, industry in the Midlands is declining, and he thinks the government should be planting as well as pruning. He doesn't believe in letting things go to seed. One way and another he's a great man for cultivating the soil. He wins prizes every year for the best council house garden in Quinton.

'He was upset,' said Nora, 'when he knew she was pregnant. So was I. She was only nineteen, and like she's always said, she didn't want to marry him.'

'I was embarrassed when she was carrying,' said Harry. 'Not when she'd had it.'

'I was never embarrassed,' protested Nora. 'Well, they're my grandchildren, aren't they?'

'All I know is,' said Harry, 'people knew about it, and it was kept secret from me.'

'All of the people I worked with, all of them knew she was going out with a coloured fellow.'

'Bar me,' Harry said. 'I never knew.'

'They accepted she was having a coloured baby.'

'They couldn't think she was having anything else, could they love?' demanded Harry.

'But I was never embarrassed,' Nora insisted.

'There was nothing to be bloody embarrassed about, was there?' said Harry. 'It was irrespective of whether it had been Japanese, Chinese, Outer Mongolian or whatever ... she was pregnant by somebody, and I look at it this way, it takes two to make a bargain. And I mean with a person like your own daughter in that predicament, what are you going to do? You're not just going to open the door and kick her out, just because she's carrying a black child. And if you look at them two kids now, how could you turn your backs on anything like that? The only difference between them two grandchildren and the others is the colour of their skins. They've got the same thoughts as me, they call me Grandad like the rest of them, they've got the run of the house like the rest of them, they get pocket money off me and all them perks, and I expect when they're grown they'll look back and they'll respect me for it, you know, irrespective of whether they're black or white. And I look at it this way, if I had ten black grandchildren, I'd rather ten perfect black children than that one of my daughters was carrying a spastic child.'

'I don't think she'll ever marry him though,' said Nora. 'She says not, any road.'

'Well, in this day and age,' Harry said, 'they pick the apple off the tree, right, and they sit back, irrespective of whether they're married or not, and let the social security take care of them. And I mean you can't blame them. I mean, if the law of the land says we'll look after that woman and child because she's single, I mean who's to blame them for going on the bandwagon. I don't say my daughter is on the bandwagon. She's only taking what she's entitled to. And I tell you this – she got no chance of an abortion, even if she was carrying a black 'un. No chance. No, the seed was planted, and why should the seed be taken away, through no fault of its own? It's not the seed's fault. Fair enough, she had it and we've looked after her. Anyway, that's the way to have children, natural. If you put a plant in the garden and it dies off, that's a bad thing, isn't it? If it comes into bloom that's a good thing, isn't it? No good saying, they should have used contraceptives, not once the seed's planted.'

He got up and looked out of the window at his roses and his chrysanthemums. A blackbird was hopping across the grass. 'And if nobody did it,' he said, 'well, there'd be nobody walking around in the world today, would there? Adam and Eve sorted that lot out, didn't they?'

Debbie lives with her little sons, Aaron and Joleon, in a council house round the corner from her mother and father. Their first home was an awful flat in a very rough area. When she went to the housing authorities and they found out she was an unmarried mother with two half-caste kiddies they stamped her file 'Problem Family' and dumped her into the worst place possible. They do that because they make assumptions. The flat was damp and Aaron had asthma and it wasn't a good time for her. She's lucky now because she's near her parents and the house is a decent size and there's a play group down the road. Her sisters have all been good to her and the house is properly furnished, though the lavatory is in the garden.

Mervyn was her first and only boyfriend. She met him while she was still at achool, when she was fifteen. Her pregnancy at nineteen was an accident, but deep down she was pleased and so was Mervyn. When her father found out he wouldn't speak to her at first. It wasn't so much that he was prejudiced, just that he was worried about what other people would think of her and the hard time she'd have coping on her own. He did tell her that she needn't get married, and she didn't want to anyway. She and Mervyn lived together for a few months but it didn't work. They played happy families for about two weeks and then it all wore off. They get on much better now that they live separately. He's unemployed and has been for six years. He lives in Aston with his mother and father. His parents both come from St Kitts and are somewhat old-fashioned in their attitudes. They're a bit like her own mother and father who still don't allow Mervyn up into her bedroom if she happens to spend the night in their house.

She doesn't 'act' black like a lot of girls who go out with coloured boys. She doesn't see the point. She's never thought of black people as different, even though she hardly saw one before she met Mervyn. Sometimes people on the street, seeing her with the children, call her a wog-lover. When she was at school the headmistress sent for her sister Beverley and hinted it was wrong for Debbie to be going out with a black boy. She implied that it was funny that someone as 'nice' as Beverley should have such a dreadful sister.

Prejudice, as far as Debbie is concerned, boils down to ignorance. The only time she's ever lost her temper over it, really seen red, was when Aaron was two and they were out shopping and she heard some skin-heads say, 'Go on, knock the black bastard over.' That made her really mad, because Aaron was so little.

The children know they're coloured. Aaron gets called Blackie at school. He tells everyone that he's coffee coloured. He calls his Auntie Judy his snowdrop and she calls him her chocolate drop. As for being married or not married, she can't see what difference it makes. Financially, she's better off the way she is. The only objection, as far as other people are concerned, must be a moral one, and morals, she says, are

~what other people think of you. She's far too much her own person to worry about what other people think. She hasn't grown like that through circumstances and having to stand on her own; she was always independent.

'I don't believe a child really needs its Dad. Not like it needs its mother. How many hours in the day does a father spend with his children? Only an hour or so. It's not as if Aaron and Joleon see less of him because he's not a permanent fixture. I do sometimes wish I'd waited until I was older to have them though. Not that nineteen is young to have kids. But I often feel that now is the time I should have started having them. I never think of meeting anyone else. Not after all this time. And I doubt if I could go with anyone else. Most white blokes wouldn't like to take on half-caste kiddies.'

She finds it easier now, being a single parent. Attitudes have changed in the last few years, though even now people who find out you have a black boyfriend immediately assume that you've been out with a whole tribe of them. She has a friend called Pam, and when they first got to know each other, Pam said, 'You must have been a real slag when you were younger.' It's ridiculous the way people say it's hard to bring up kids on your own. It isn't exactly a bunch of roses, not until you get the money and the housing difficulties sorted out, but it's easy after that, particularly when they're no longer babies. Everyone thinks it has to be hard, because where would men fit in if it wasn't?

*

Debbie's right, you know. It is easy for a woman to look after children. It should be what she's best at. It's coping with men that's difficult, and maybe if your childhood family is a close-knit one and supportive, and the State is on your side, there's really no need to grapple with the complexities of an extended family. Men don't have that much power over women any more, not as husbands that is, because economically they've become superfluous. But where does that leave the children? I don't really approve of single-parent families – I've been one myself for years. It's all right for people with strong convictions and strong connections to go out on a limb, but what about those teenage girls filed away under 'Problem Families', those inheritors of sub-standard housing who have neither the experience nor the common sense to look after their babies properly?

I was musing on this while travelling through an area of Birmingham which seemed to be entirely populated by Asians and West Indians. If nothing else Birmingham is a multiracial city and nobody seems upset about it, just so long as people keep to their own neck of the woods. We passed an Indian girl on the way to her wedding, decked out like a princess with rose petals in her hair and golden sandals on her feet. Her mother scurried behind; her father strode ahead, portly and important. There were some English guests following at a distance with carnations in their buttonholes, but I doubt if the groom was British. Asian girls don't have the same choices, they're still brought up in a patriarchal society. This particular princess would be handed from father to husband like a bunch of flowers.

When I was younger I would have disapproved of such a system, but age makes one reactionary, and like an old horse knowing its way home I veer more and more to the right. It's not only age. I went to an Indian wedding two years ago and it seemed an admirable way of securing a lasting union. The couple had been married at a ceremony which had taken place three months before, but had not yet cohabited. Their final bonding, the sealing of the contract, took place on the stage of a school hall in Finchley. The bride and groom sat facing one another with a table-cloth draped between them so that they couldn't gaze into each other's eyes. The priest, in a pair of baggy trousers which kept slipping down – for religious reasons he was not allowed to wear either belt or braces – skipped round them shouting hoarsely and bursting coloured balloons tied to the corners of the fair-ground canopy under which they sat. The relatives of the couple sat on either side, watching and commenting loudly on the scene. Small children rolled across the stage. The audience, some three hundred people, alternately shouted encouragement or went off to queue in the school canteen for paper plates dolloped with helpings of curry and sweetmeats. It was explained to me that the complicated ritual I was watching brought the bride into the circle of the groom's parents, brothers, uncles, grandfathers and ancestors. She was marrying a family rather than an individual. A fire was eventually lit in a steel bucket and, the table-cloth being symbolically torn down, the couple rose and walked seven times round the flames, holding hands and singing. After three hours they went home for a rest and then came back for a quiet dinner for two behind the curtain on the stage. Then at midnight they returned to the home of the groom's parents, a bungalow in Cricklewood, and retired for the first time as man and wife. They would live in the house for as long as it took to train them in the arts of cooking and husbandship and rubbing along together. Then, when they were thought capable and experienced enough to live alone, a house would be bought for them. It seems a sensible arrangement and likely to lead to one of permanence, though that is not to say that a brisk canter through the registry office, a ham and pork-pie breakfast and ten days in sunny Benidorm cannot achieve the same result.

I was on my way to visit Sam Lescott, Mervyn's father, grandfather of Debbie's children. He works for a paint manufacturer, mixing colours. I knew that Mrs Lescott was away in St Kitts attending a funeral, and I was shy of meeting her husband. I didn't mind meeting Mervyn – I classed him as one of the children, alongside Debbie and my own offspring – but Mr Lescott and I were of the same generation.

Prejudice is planted in childhood, learnt like table manners and cadences of speech, nurtured through fictions like *Uncle Tom's Cabin* and *Gone with the Wind*. It's inherent in brand names and images – the gollywog on the marmalade jar, the nigger minstrel show at the end of the pier. Thirty years ago my Auntie Margo, seeing me reading *The Mill on the Floss*, asked me who had written it. When I told her she said, 'My word, I never knew the chocolate covered coon wrote books.' She had gone to school from the age of seven to the age of ten, and in that brief span she learned to read, to add up and to write in copperplate. The rest of her learning – not to tell lies, to trust in God – came from Sunday school at St Emmanuel's in Anfield. While she was at school a teacher broke the nose of a little girl who had failed to memorise her catechism. My Auntie Nellie had never forgotten it, just as she had never forgotten the missionary who talked to them about the heathens in Africa, the savages in the jungle.

Black men like Sam Lescott arrived here after the war with their characters and their dispositions already coloured by assumptions. If they weren't religious like Uncle Tom, or comic like those grinning faces stamped on cocoa tins, they were somehow sinister and brutish. It had something to do with sex, deep down, though God knows where that came from. Maybe it's because they were thought of as animals, and that must have come in part from people like Livingstone and his travels in Africa. I remember my mother, a mild soul in many ways, coming home from shopping in Liverpool and telling my father that she had just bought some cut-price shoelaces from a 'big buck negro' in the market. A buck, being a male of the species, has something in common with the stallion. My mother, who didn't much care for that side of things, would have been hard pressed to explain what she meant by such a sentence. My father, on the other hand, had been raised to believe that Catholics were worse than bugs, and considered the Pope on a par with Hitler, closely followed by Churchill. And foreigners weren't much better, but there again it may have been a sexual prejudice – all papists bred like rabbits and all continentals were sex maniacs. I'm not sure where Winston fitted in. Oddly enough, my father approved of Jews and was often mistaken for one, and when he was labelled as such he didn't deny it but took it on the nose.

I never spoke to any black people when I was growing up in Liverpool, though there were plenty in the streets. They were part of the lower classes, like the Irish. They didn't have to be warned against because they were so far down the social scale as to be invisible. People who didn't talk nicely or who drank were far more dangerous; they were everywhere and could actually infiltrate into the home since they could be living next door or over the road. The Chinese were a bit of a puzzle. They looked inferior but they were very clean and tended to make money. I'm talking about the 1940s, of course, those dark ages, and things have changed since then. My own children say that in my head I appear to regard everyone as equal, yet they sense my hidden prejudices. But then, youth is a storehouse. It's not just some quirk of the mind that makes old people forget what they did yesterday and yet remember in detail the events of a day in childhood. Being a child lasts for ever; the rest of life soars past on wings. My children, faced with someone with a German sounding name, will possibly feel revulsion; nothing logical, simply a gut response learnt from a mother who had been taught that the Germans had butchered the Jews.

When I arrived at the house, Mervyn and his father were about to sit down to their evening meal. There was a delicious smell coming from the kitchen and a glimpse of a long table spread with a white cloth. I asked Sam if he had minded when Debbie got pregnant.

'Me? No,' he said, looking baffled. 'Why should I mind?'

'But if one of your daughters got pregnant by a white man and he wouldn't marry her, wouldn't you have minded then?'

'No,' he said. He didn't look me in the eye and I wasn't convinced.

'Debbie doesn't want to get married,' Mervyn said, 'any more than I do. I don't want to get tied down.'

'And you haven't got a job?' I said. It sounded like an accusation.

'No,' he said. 'I did have one once for two years, but it wasn't getting me anywhere. I suppose I could get a job, some sort of job, but then why should I work for £35 a week knowing that the man next to me is getting £135 a week for the same job?'

'You wouldn't think of moving to London either?'

'No. Why should I? It's more stable here. People in Brum are more integrated than down South. There's not the same sort of trouble here.'

'When I first came here,' said Sam, 'we were some of the first to come. We never had a lot of trouble. But since then there's been another generation. A lot of trouble today is caused by the younger generation. It doesn't just happen to us. I know from some of the parents in the paint shop where I work, the English parents, that they're having the same sort of trouble with their young. When we had the riots ...'

'The riots were bound to happen,' said Mervyn. 'You see, they're all unemployed, unless they're pushing real hard stuff and there's a lot of big money in it and if you try to clamp down there's bound to be trouble. The riots started because some of the police – I'm not saying all – but some, were in it too, and maybe they stopped getting paid off, so they clamped down because they weren't getting their money no more, and then there was trouble. And next time it'll be guns.'

'You've got a different generation of police too,' his father said.

'The majority of pushers are black,' Mervyn said, 'but then the punters are white – so where do you draw the line?'

I asked if he was worried about the future for Aaron and Joleon. What did he want for them?

'I want the best,' he said. 'I mean, I'll tell them they've got to work at school, like my parents told me. My brothers and sisters all got jobs. I'm the only one who hasn't in this family. But I don't think it's going to be easy for them.'

*

'If you're very good,' crooned Debbie, 'if you're really, really good, Mummy will bring you back a pressie.' She was squatting down and cuddling Joleon who didn't want to let her go.

'Are these his clothes?' asked Beverley, picking up a carrier bag from the sofa. She was taking Joleon home to her house for the weekend. Aaron was going to stay in Aston with Mervyn, at his grandparents' house. The girls, Judy and Diane, Jackie and Debbie, were going on a bus trip to Weston-super-Mare. Their Mum was going too and their Auntie; they'd been saving up for it for months. It wasn't Beverley's sort of thing.

Beverley is buying her own house, with a friend. She left school at sixteen and went to Hallesowen College to do her O levels. After that she joined the WRAC. She was brought up in an old-fashioned home – they were put to work on Sundays, two to clean upstairs, two to dust below, and Debbie scrubbing out the kitchen with Mother. They all made their own beds. When she was small, Beverley used to sing through a comb to amuse the family. It probably had something to do with her father, him being on the Halls with Florrie Ford. Judy used to blow tunes through the spout of a Crown Derby teapot. Not that Judy was always so entertaining – she was a skin-head when she was a teenager and wore bovver boots. She shaved her head and when she spoke to them all she ever said was 'Drop dead.'

While she was in the kitchen looking for Joleon's juice

cup, I asked Beverley what she had felt when she'd known that Debbie was going to have a black baby.

'She's family,' she said. 'I love them all and I wouldn't want any of them to be different. Maybe prejudice comes from people like me. It's not easy having black in the family. I used to go down town and see the sort of girls who went out with coloured boys. The way they dressed, the way they spoke, they looked like tarts. They were aping themselves. I didn't want Debbie to be classed with them. Debbie's never had any prejudice whatever. Never. She's accepted by black people. She has lots of black friends. They don't think of her as white. And it's not that she acts black, not like some of them do. She's very straight, our Debbie. If she doesn't take to you, she tells you so straight out. She's dead forward.'

'Hurry up,' called Judy. 'We'll miss the bus.'

'Where's his food?' asked Beverley, joking, poking about in the carrier bag. 'You know he eats like a pig.'

'Give Mummy a kiss,' said Debbie, holding out her arms to Aaron.

The bus was a double-decker with a bar down below. 'Act natural,' shouted Judy, swanning across the parking lot and jumping aboard. They all sat together on the top deck, the sisters and Mum and Auntie. It's not as if they don't see each other every day. But then, they like each other. They're a tangled bouquet, these Roses.

It was out of the ordinary, as bus rides go. We played Bingo and drank double vodkas. The intercom-system linking us to below deck was on the blink and the Bingo caller kept shouting, 'Hallo, hallo ...' and every time he said it, no matter how many times, we all sang back, 'Who's your lady-friend? Who's the little girlie by your side?' It never stopped being funny. There was a lady in charge of a bucket who fined anyone who swore. The money was to be used to buy a drink for the driver. Even before we started we had enough to buy half a barrel.

The Bingo caller was West Indian and wore a

pink-spotted bowler hat. He stood on the stairs, grinning and shouting the numbers – 'All the fours, forty-four. Number ten, Maggie's den.' 'Boo,' we yelled, and worse, and the lady with the bucket ran up the aisle collecting the fines.

We drove along the motorway through Worcestershire and Gloucestershire and hardly looked out of the window. Our throats were hoarse, and Debbie's auntie won on the Bingo. Nora Rose was sitting in a fog of cigarette smoke, not coughing for once. Someone passed round a cartoon of Prince Charles and Diana. Charles hadn't got his trousers on and Diana was holding a beer bottle. It was growing dark. Old Somerset was ahead, and a chip supper and a nocturnal sprint beside the briny towards the nearest pub.

I didn't enjoy my night. I was too shy to join everyone for supper and stayed in my room. It was the size of a broom cupboard and I couldn't open the wardrobe door and sit on the bed at the same time. The television set had a slot meter and in the middle of a film the money ran out. Revellers ran up and down the corridors into the small hours, singing and shouting.

*

In the morning I went out onto the front with my guide book and walked along the shore, keeping my distance from the motorbikes, bucking like broncos, that wheeled beside the briny. If I turned my back to the waves I could see the lump of the prehistoric encampment to the east, and the heights of Uphill to the west. Uphill, I read, the sea-breezes flickering the pages of my book, was originally called Hubba's Pill, the latter word being a corruption of the Briton/Welsh word for pool formed by the estuary of the Axe. Hubba was a Danish pirate who raided the coast. He was slain in battle at a place called Bloody Corner near Appledore, Devonshire, in 882, while fighting Alfred the Great – the fellow who was making arrows while the cakes turned black. I couldn't see the remains of Worspring Priory established by Fitz-Urse, one of the knights who did for Thomas à Becket. It didn't really bother me; it was interesting but irrelevent. Above the hiss of the sea rose the roar of the combustion engines as the piratical ton-up boys of Somerset rode their bikes across the wet and dimpled sands

Later that morning I went into the centre of the town with the Rose girls to visit the joke shop. Someone bought a plastic turd which was very lifelike, and Judy had a photo taken of herself with Dracula teeth and blood dripping down her chin. She wanted to borrow the turd for good measure, but Jackie said she was disgusting.

Debbie bought Joleon's present at the shop next door. He'd asked for a billiard table but he was getting a stick of rock. Diane and Jackie and I went to a cafe for a cup of coffee. Debbie and Judy sat at another table, pretending not to listen.

'I know,' said Jackie, 'that she's getting on great now, but it's still hard bringing up children on your own. I was the first to know that she was pregnant, like – and I wouldn't change either Aaron or Joleon, but it isn't practical, is it, bringing up kids on your own? I mean, she had a good job ...'

'And she had to give it up,' Jackie said.

'And it's only now,' Diane said, 'in these last few months, that Debbie is as she is. I mean, before that she let herself go – she hadn't a man to help her, had she?'

'Just because you've got kids,' said Jackie, 'it doesn't mean you should let yourself go.'

'I mean, I've always had Paddy when the kids were ill,' Diane said.

'She hadn't got that, had she?', said Jackie.

'And she couldn't see it, could she?' Diane said. 'Cos she wasn't at that age. I mean, she couldn't see that she couldn't have my house and furniture at 31 when she was only 21.'

'She wanted what we've got,' Jackie said.

'And she couldn't have it, could she?' said Diane. 'She couldn't see ...'

'She's very stubborn,' explained Jackie, shaking her head.

'That what we've got you have to wait for,' said Diane. 'I waited seventeen years.'

'And she couldn't wait, could she?'

'I've got to give her credit,' Diane said. 'She's done it all by herself. I know we've helped, but really it's been down to her. I mean, she drives me crackers, but she's a strong person and we can't take any credit for what she's done.'

'Not really,' said Jackie. 'She's a law unto herself.'

'Maybe if she hadn't had the family round her she wouldn't have been able to do it,' Diane said. 'I don't know. But I assure you, what Debbie wants, she gets.'

'Oh, she does,' Jackie agreed. 'She does.'

In the evening there was a fancy dress parade in the dining-room. It was the highlight of the weekend. Judy was a third of the Beverley Sisters, dressed up in a yellow wig and wearing an army uniform. They mimed 'Don't sit under the Apple Tree' to a gramophone record with a mop stuck up in front of them to represent a microphone. You could tell that Judy had grease paint in her veins. The driver of the bus was the compère of the show, rigged out like Jack Buchanan in top hat and tails. He had a difficult job, choosing who should win the fancy dress. There was a mad aviator with wings, a perverted dwarf with a joke shop nose, a Vera Duckworth with a plastic bosom exposed, as though she'd had a rough night out at the Rover's Return, a Ronnie Corbett in short pants and a schoolboy hat, several male fairies in bloomers carrying suggestive wands, and two black and white minstrels, the white blacked up and the black chalked white. The success of the evening, however, was the Cock of the North, his kilt tucked up and a phallus as big as a yard-arm jerking flamboyantly to the beat of the band as he paraded between a fairy and the King of Siam.

It was a good night out, as they say, and had more in

common with an England of the past than of the present. Never mind that the decor of the lounge-cum-dining-room with its mass-produced carpeting, its plastic veneer woodwork, its lavatory notices in neon lights, its tables set with everlasting tulips, with pepper pots shaped like Miss Piggy, salt cellars coned like missiles, was horrendously up to date. For once, the telly was turned off and we were entertaining ourselves, playing the fool, acting the clown.

Nora and Debbie sat at a table to one side, out of the spotlight. The lady who had earlier organised the swear box was taking photographs. In the years to come, what will the Rose family remember when they look at the snapshots in the album? Will the camera merely have recorded the laughter on the faces, the beauty spots and the funny hats, or will it have captured by some miracle of emotion and sensitivity, the subliminal web of love and concern which caught Debbie and her children in its threads so long ago?

*

On my last day in Birmingham I went to say goodbye to Mr and Mrs Rose. Aaron and Joleon were on the swing in the garden, swooshing through the sunshine above the roses. How sweet, I thought. How innocent. Who in their right mind could treat one child differently from another on account of colour? Who indeed? But what about when they're grown, when the same adjectives won't apply, and they won't be playing safely in the garden?

Harry Rose had the last word, though he didn't answer my question.

'They let them immigrants come in, which you can't blame; they were asked to come in, they were brought in, they were transported in. They've got families of their own now and they've intermarried, and them two thousand or so who were here in the middle fifties have expanded to thousands and thousands. And as long as there's stars in the sky these people will still be here. No good Maggie Thatcher or these other people offering them money to go home – they were born here, they were bred here, they're black and they're British.'

Epilogue

At night, during the war, within the cavernous waiting room of Central Station, young girls, their legs smeared with damp sand to imitate stockings, flicked their eyebrows with fingers dipped in vaseline and swarmed out into the dim stretch of Stanley Street to where, white puttees gleaming, batons swinging on leather straps, the American military police patrolled the streets of Liverpool. Mimicking their swagger, begging for cigarettes and gum, the children ran behind, legs pocked with the marks of insect bites. A smell clung to them, a mixture of dirt and vermin and the cloying odour of damp rags. Even in winter they ran barefoot.

The North I knew as a child, although in decline, managed to find employment for a majority of its inhabitants. And yet the expectations of that majority, its standards of housing, of education, were hardly different from those of a century before. The urchins who roamed the streets were not forerunners of that hippy, happy generation who twined flowers in their hair, but continuing spectres of Victorian England, waifs and vagrants who in their turn produced another generation of disadvantaged citizens.

The war forced changes, not least in the rebuilding of houses. The city council launched into an orgy of bulldozing, flattening areas missed by the Luftwaffe. The architects designed their high-rise estates. Before the grand redevelopment scheme could be completed the money ran out.

Forty years on, disfigured by office blocks and precincts, by ring roads and fly-overs, the city I knew has all but disappeared. Gone the cobblestones and the tramlines, the overhead railway and Exchange Station, St John's Market and the Cabbage Hall. They have obliterated the terraced houses, burnt down the Rialto, turned the warehouses into museums, the foreshore into a garden, torn the angels and the tombstones from the graveyard of the Cathedral. The ships have left the river.

The same could be said for every other industrial city in the North. Their inhabitants are better off, no doubt of that, being neither starved nor overworked, oppressed by priests or crushed by class. The south too has altered, but this was due to agricultural rather than industrial change, and the results cannot be compared.

All the families in this book are directly linked to that generation of men and women who were children during the First World War, inheritors of the depression which inevitably followed, participants in a second war of equal inevitability, beneficiaries of a Welfare State, of technological and medical advances the like of which the world had previously only dreamed of. While it survives, that hung generation dangling between a brutal past and an unsettled present, the assumptions, the bitterness, the misconceptions remain.

Perhaps only when that older generation – North and South – has finally disappeared will the concept of a divided nation fade. Until then, we can't live in the past, but those who choose either to ignore it or forget it may well be condemned to relive it in the future.